To Sardino Family

This book is a reminder of
the friends you made in
Australia.

Love
Elizabeth xx
10-12-1974

The pathways of life are so many
So as from each other we stray.
Here's just a few lines to remind you,
Of the friends that you met on the way.

The Red Centre

The Red Centre

Robin Smith text by Keith Willey

RIGBY

Contents

ACKNOWLEDGEMENT

So many people gave their help during the production of this book that it would be impossible to mention them all by name.

For assistance with the revised edition I would like to thank Mrs Iris Harvey and Mr Ted Marron of Alice Springs.

Robin Smith

RIGBY LIMITED
Adelaide Sydney Melbourne Perth Brisbane
First published 1967
Revised and enlarged edition published 1974
National Library of Australia Registry Card Number
and ISBN 0 85179 777 6
Printed in Hong Kong

The Monolith in the Desert

CENTRAL AUSTRALIA IS a barren, timeless land. Windswept rock hills rear in folds on the border of a wide open plain. Cliffs, smoothed humps of granite, canyons with here and there a pool of water glinting from some deep cleft . . . It is a harsh landscape, where lightly-timbered cattle country can change utterly in a mile to a surface red as rusted metal and bare as the surface of the moon.

Geologically the Centre is said to be one of the oldest parts of the earth's crust. And, as is customary with great age, its arteries have hardened and dried up. When rains do come, the ancient, eroded rivers—the Finke and the Todd, and all the others which scar the land with their spidery pattern—fill, burst their banks and spread through the country.

After a brief rampage they peter out in the desert sands south of Alice. Pools of moisture quickly disappear, leaving only marks on the plain which soon will be baked hard. For most of the time the creekbeds are arid, dead; mere ghosts of what rivers should be. The nearest permanent streams to Alice Springs in the territory are the Katherine and the Roper more than 1000 kilometres to the north. Because of this, water is always a problem, and a talking-point wherever Centralians gather.

The inland is dangerous country for newcomers. Even today you could perish only half an hour by

LEFT: *Ayers Rock, the world's mightiest monolith, is over 8 kilometres around and rises 348.3 metres above the surrounding plain.*

BELOW: *During the rare flood times rivers spread over the plain, then recede quickly, scoring the earth with an intricate pattern of stream beds.*

Columns made of natural stone form the gateway to Ayers Rock-Mount Olga National Park.

car from Alice Springs itself. The sun, generating temperatures of 43 degrees and more, and the excessively dry atmosphere, can dehydrate a lost man, leaving a blackened corpse within forty-eight hours. Once off the main road the traveller's safety depends largely on the efficiency of modern transport and communications. When these fail he may find himself in a difficult and dangerous situation: the radio develops a fault that only an expert can repair; the truck breaks a tailshaft or strips the teeth of the differential; the plane has a choke in a fuel pipe or runs out of petrol before its pilot can reach a scheduled landing ground. Incidents like these can throw you on your own resources at a moment's notice; can maroon the city-dweller at some lonely spot a hundred kilometres or more from outside assistance, pitted against the cruelty of the desert.

Yet there is something about the Centre which draws visitors from afar. Maybe it is the sense of adventure latent in all of us. Even from the seat of a tourist coach, with air-conditioning and every convenience modern technology can provide, it would be a dull traveller who could not absorb something of the immensity, the silence and the brooding challenge of inland Australia.

The scenery alone is a lifetime experience. The red cliffs, the rare waterholes, cold and clear and deep; the primordial splendour of a landscape like no other on earth—these things stay long in the memory.

Out in the desert, more than 300 kilometres south-west of Alice Springs, is the mightiest spectacle of all—Ayers Rock, a single enormous boulder three and a half kilometres long, one and a half kilometres wide, and rising 348.3 metres above the surrounding plain. This natural monolith has been described with justice as one of the wonders of the world. Long ago the Loritjas venerated it as "Oolera", a sacred Dreaming Place. Now the ragged remnants of the tribe, riding their camels far to the west where even the nomad Pintubis seldom venture and trailed by their retinue of dogs, usually keep well clear of the Rock. It is Oolera no more. The white man has taken over, roaring to and fro in his aeroplanes and cars, clicking camera shutters by the thousand; littering the weird humped crest with picnic debris and scrawled initials.

W. C. Gosse, who discovered the Rock on July 17, 1873, and named it after a premier of South Australia, expressed his amazement at the spectacle. He wrote: "When I was only two miles distant and the hill, for the first time, coming fairly into view, what was my astonishment to find it was an immense pebble, rising abruptly from the plain . . . This rock is certainly the most wonderful natural feature I have seen."

It is the world's biggest monolith, a great mould of sandstone measuring more than 8 kilometres round the base, set in some of the most inhospitable country in the Centre. No stock live within a day's walk of the Rock. Yet the rare thunderstorms can transform the wasteland into a garden of flowers and rich green pasture.

People overseas who have never heard of Brisbane or Adelaide know of the Rock. Its strange aura of majesty and great age has done more than any other feature of the Centre to draw the tourists north. Each year more than 40,000 visitors cross the desert by aircraft or four-wheel-drive vehicle just to gaze at the monolith.

Ayers Rock looms on the horizon from afar as a thin wraith-like outline. Soon it is unmistakable,

Ayers Rock is a photographer's delight altering its moods according to the aspect and time of day. Low sunlight over terra-cotta coloured sands in ripples create interesting conditions.

a primaeval monster, unaffected by the huddle of tourist chalets and vehicles at its base. From a distance the surface appears smooth as glass but a closer inspection shows it is pitted enough to give rubber-soled shoes or sandshoes a good grip. The western face slopes a little less steeply than the other approaches, and here the more athletic visitors climb to the top, walking straight up the face, with head and shoulders thrust well forward, like a column of venturesome ants.

The summit, a wide lumpy expanse of stone, is topped at its highest point by a cairn with a bronze disc detailing distances of surrounding features. Clearly visible to the west are the Olgas, a cluster of mammoth boulders, some even taller than the

Rock, though lacking its great bulk.

On the summit of Ayers Rock a few scraggy bushes and even trees manage somehow to maintain life. Dotted about are round holes pitted in the stone, some eight to ten feet deep and filled with water. Years ago several of the pools were regarded as permanent and even contained tiny fish which the aborigines called *kundje-kundje*. These perished when the water dried up completely during the recent drought, but wallaby and rabbit droppings show that even in this barren place a few hardy animals survive.

At ground level 11 kilometres of road completely encircle the Rock, which is a monster of varying moods and many facets. There is the Sound

*Tourists tackling "The Climb" on the
north-west corner of Ayers Rock.*

RIGHT: *Water dripping through the sandstone has formed these
stalactites pointing down from the roof of the Women's Cave —
one of the many caverns which honeycomb Ayers Rock.*

Shell, a hollowed cavity shaped in flowing lines as if formed by the action of the sea. Actually it is the result of wind erosion through thousands of centuries. A heavy breeze makes a weird sighing noise inside it. In the old days the Aborigines thought this was the voice of spirits, and after nightfall they always moved well away into the mulga.

Other features of the monolith include the Brain—an eroded wall honeycombed and shaped like a human brain—and the Kangaroo Tail, a 150 metre strip of stone hanging down one end of Ayers Rock with sunlight glinting through the gap in between. In many places are clefts and subterranean grottoes whose walls are covered with native paintings which rank from genuine "Dreaming" motifs to what can only be described as "Stone Age doodling".

The importance Oolera held in tribal life is easily understood. Apart from the spiritual significance which such an example of Nature's artistry was sure to attract, a big pool, Maggie Springs, nestles at the base of the Rock. This was the most reliable waterhole in thousands of square kilometres and in dry times the tribes must have fought many a desperate battle for its possession. The steep face of Mutjilda Gorge, above the springs, looks unscalable. Yet that is the way Gosse and his Afghan companion Kamran went up in 1873.

The monolith is a photographer's delight, altering its mood according to the aspect and time of day. The colour changes through all the shades from fiery red to a delicate mauve. Some years ago an entranced visitor wrote: "Nearby were the terracotta red sandhills, relieved by the grey of the solanums and the eremphilas; stretching out before us was a wide sandy flat, spotted with dark-foliaged desert oaks and covered so thickly with spinifex in seed that it resembled a wheat field ready for the harvest, and ten miles away, resting on the waterless billows of sand like a great leviathan, was the great red Rock."

During the terrible dry years extending from the late 1950s to 1965—"the worst drought in the time of the white man", as one veteran Centralian called it—vegetation around Ayers Rock received a severe and perhaps irreparable setback. A warning was given early in 1963 by Colonel Lionel Rose, one-time Director of Animal Industry for the Northern Territory. He said people who had visited the

Visitors to Ayers Rock stream up the rock like a trail of ants. Most people find the climb strenuous but a hardy Scotsman is said to have blown his bagpipes all the way.

Rock area over the previous fifteen years were horrified at the effect of prolonged drought on the tree cover.

The land for about a mile around the monolith had always carried a fair covering of trees and shrubs. In 1963 two-thirds of the mulgas and witcheties were dead. The one permanent watering-place at the base of the Rock, Maggie Springs, was nearly dry. Colonel Rose speculated that this might be due either to inadequate replenishment from the Rock's huge catchment area or to a lowering of the water level by two bores sunk three-quarters of a mile away by the tourist developers.

The tree cover on the fixed red sandhills beyond the near perimeter of Ayers Rock was almost solely Desert Oak. Seventy per cent of these graceful and long-lived trees were either dead or so denuded of their foliage that they were unlikely to grow again.

Colonel Rose discussed the position with the Animal Industry Branch botanist, George Chippendale, who considered the succession of drought years had caused irreparable damage. There is a suggestion that our arid zones are becoming slowly more arid, and such damage may be beyond the capacity of man to prevent or overcome.

Unlike other parts of the drought area in Central Australia which were stocked with cattle—overstocked, some said—neither man nor beast could be blamed for the desolation and tree mortality around the Rock. Nor did there appear to be any solution to the problem, which was aggravated by the fact that even the hardy spinifex was dead or dying. Colonel Rose said: "This means we may even see the spectre of the fixed sandhills being windswept and moved unless rain and some sort of holding cover precedes a succession of high winds."

Events since may have proved him too gloomy a prophet. But while good rains since 1966 have brought a profuse growth of pasture and wildflowers, the scrub itself is slow to recover. Even where new trees are sprouting they will take many years to reach their former stature.

The recurrent droughts when even the kangaroos die in thousands pose the question: How did the Aborigines survive so long in this country? Why did they come out here in the first place?

The late Bill Braitling of Mount Doreen station had an intriguing theory that the conventional picture of a Stone Age migration pressing down from the tropics and reaching right out into deserts where no other human being could—or would want to—live, was a false one. He asked: "How could primitive men, wandering from the tropical north into a desert with wooden spears and throwing sticks for their only weapons, succeed in adapt-

The Centre is a land of contrast. During the long dry spells the road to Ayers Rock is very deep in dust.

LEFT: *At the highest point of Ayers Rock is a cairn where a bronze disc details distances and directions to surrounding features.*

ABOVE: *Ayers Rock at sunrise.*

LEFT: *The red earth plain which stretches away from the monolith in every direction seems inhospitable to life. Yet it can become a carpet of flowers after rain.*

RIGHT: *Ramparts of rock, rising like storm-tossed waves. The scene is Mount Conner. It might as easily be the surface of the moon.*

A rare sight as rain collected on the broad summit of the Rock cascades down the face in a series of waterfalls. Wind and water have combined through the centuries to erode the monolith into fantastic shapes.

ing themselves to such arid conditions? Accustomed only to the lush northlands, how could they have survived in country that will hardly support a dingo?"

Braitling's answer was that their links with the Centre went back much farther in time than anyone had imagined—perhaps a million years. He believed that they arrived in the area when an inland sea still covered much of what is now arid plain; when palm trees nodded by a silent shore and the diprotodon and other monsters now extinct wandered the jungle. Slowly, inch by inch and foot by foot, the sea dried up, the rivers ceased flowing, the foliage withered. The diprotodon vanished from the earth, leaving his petrified bones, along with shells, fossils and marine relics, for scientists of later centuries to ponder. But

smaller, hardier animals survived. So did the Aborigine.

Braitling believed they never had to go out into the desert to find their soaks. They knew where they were. For generations they had watched the destruction of a fertile countryside. As the waters dwindled the tribes moved with them, setting the pattern for later migrations and "walkabouts". And when the last billabongs gave out they followed the water down by burrowing deep into the ground.

For his theory to be correct the Aborigine would have had to be longer in Australia than even the most daring scientist has yet imagined. The impermanence of most of their relics, the lack of buildings or even of many implements that could stand the test of time, make it impossible to gauge how long.

Certain it is, however, that they had been adrift from the mainstream of humanity since an age long past. Some indication of the length of time the Aborigine has been in Australia has been gained in two recent discoveries. Archeologists have dated a female skeleton found at Lake Mungo near Broken Hill in 1969 as being 26,000 years old. In 1968 a number of skeletons with very primitive features were found at Kow Swamp in the Murray Valley. These have been dated at between 10,000 and 20,000 years old.

Meanwhile remains of the inland sea still linger —vast saltpans where mirages glimmer in the distance with a promise of water and vegetation which is all too seldom realised. Lakes Eyre, Frome, Torrens, Callabonna, Mackay, Amadeus . . . there are many of them.

Even Ayers Rock may be the final vestige of a high plateau which covered much of the Centre and, through the ages, has been worn away elsewhere by the erosion of wind and rain. Whatever its history, we know the monolith has stood in its place for an unimaginable span of years. When, perhaps, Alice Springs has gone, Ayers Rock still will remain, mighty in size, altering so slowly that a million years would make little discernible difference, dwarfing man and his efforts to change a timeless land.

The Ayers Rock—Mount Olga area is a national park and the Northern Territory Administration

An old Aborigine — one of the few still living near Ayers Rock — sits inside one of the rock's caves and looks out over the surrounding plains.

has appointed a series of Rangers to ensure there is no desecration of a great natural asset. The first and best-remembered of these "Keepers of the Rock" was the late Bill Harney, poet, raconteur, and bush cook extraordinary. If true wealth is measured by the friends a man leaves behind him the eloquent old bushman was rich indeed. When he died in 1963 his mourners throughout the nation numbered thousands, for, as befitted one of the moulders of the Australian legend, Bill had a rare talent for mateship. In accordance with his wish he was laid to rest at Mount Buderim cemetery near Mooloolaba, Queensland.

"Billarney" as he was to Territorians had no peer as a storyteller. Yet those twinkling blue eyes and the darting humour masked an inner tragedy which he never inflicted on his friends. Occasionally it come out in his poetry:

> Mid bai a gi ri mana, hear, oh hear,
> Upon the winds of life my song is thrown
> Till grass and tree each shed a dewy tear;
> The world is glad today, yet I'm alone.

Though he had his full measure of human lusts and failings, Bill looked out on life honestly and with clarity. There was about him a quality, almost of innocence, which left no place in his world for trickery and double-dealing. When he left his cattle station at Borroloola in the twenties he made a present of it to a friend. He did the same with the house he built in Darwin at the end of World War Two. It would not have occurred to him to ask for payment.

Bill Harney was sixty-seven. His part-Aboriginal wife Linda and children Beattie and Billy predeceased him years before. Instead of a family he left behind his writings—eight books, each dealing with natives and the bush; each a treasure-house of reading for future generations of men and women who may inhabit a very different kind of Australia from the brave, simple one Bill Harney knew.

He left school at nine, after only three and a half years of formal education. Yet I believe his poetry at least, much of it written in association with A. P. Elkin, will endure when many other works which are acclaimed by the literary world today have vanished.

> The Dreamtime heroes move; like phantoms deep
> From distant ages—fleeting shapes that leap
> Upon the black man's thoughts; each one recalls
> Creek or river, springs or waterfalls
> Within his tribal lands—from first to last
> Recording deeds of heroes in the past.
> Thus does the black man breathe again the air

> Of Pakadringa, rain-man, and his care;
> Of Totem-heroes out of whom tribes leapt
> When Thunder-giants fought and Lightnings swept
> Throughout the land—to all a warning clear
> To follow the path they trod, the way austere
> Of Dawn-folk springing from the misty past
> From Dreamtime nights, when life on earth was cast.

Bill Harney, a short stocky man with a face as cracked and weathered as the territory outback he knew so well, was born in Charters Towers, Queensland. He served with the first A.I.F., was wounded at Gallipoli, later fought in France and was mentioned in despatches.

In 1919, to "get away from it all", he came to the territory, where he worked and lived among the Aborigines for forty years. He was a drover, cattleman, miner, fencer, trader, and Native Affairs Patrol Officer. He was a member of, and adviser to, the Arnhem Land expeditions of 1948, 1951 and 1952, and the Melville Island expedition of 1955.

Bill entered the profession of authorship, which was to bring him world-wide acclaim, almost by accident. He was on Melville Island in 1934-35. As he put it: "For six months I had no book to read. But I had a lot of paper. So I wrote one." But, in the Territory at least, Bill's fame rested as much on his abilities as a "poisoner" or bush cook, as on his writings. He could whip up a meal out of practically anything. *Bill Harney's Cook Book* was a delight to read, though as a guide to city gourmets it was handicapped by the difficulty of obtaining such ingredients as snakes, flying foxes and lizards.

Bill was especially fond of witchetty grubs, which he compared with the large white snails and edible frogs of France. "They can be eaten raw," he wrote, "but in my opinion they are nicer cooked. They should be cooked on clean, white ashes from a wood fire till they are crisp. They have a very nice flavour, difficult to describe, but which perhaps is a little like egg. All you do is cut them out of the tree and cook over the coals. But in a frying pan, with a dab of butter, they have an extra flavour." Bill often wondered, rather sadly, why so few Australians ate grubs. But he accepted the national aversion philosophically: "If no-one had seen an oyster before the white man came out here,

From a distance the mighty monolith looks smooth like a water-worn pebble.

how many of us would be eating them today?"

After many years of knocking about in the North Bill "sat down" at a camp on Two-Feller Creek near Darwin. There he stayed until 1957, when he announced that Darwin had become "too civilised" and went off to the Centre to become the Keeper of Ayers Rock.

For four years he had charge at the Rock, entertaining thousands of visitors with his tales of the bush and old times. His renown as a raconteur became so great that the BBC put him on a record. "They actually PAID me for talking," an amazed Harney told his mates. He retired in 1962 on a Commonwealth Literary Fund grant to write about the camel-riding Loritjas of the desert.

Several months before his death he severed links with the territory, which had brought him much heartbreak and some fame, and returned to his native Queensland. "I'm going down to Mooloolaba where you can put a plant in the ground and watch it come up green," he said.

Billarney made mates wherever he went and he never lacked an audience in Mooloolaba. But the territory, though he left it at the end, was his real home. There he is loved and remembered by all who knew him. Perhaps the best epitaph comes from his "Songs of the Songmen":

Poor fellow me,
Poor fellow me,
My country
It gave me
All that I see,
Gifts that I see,
All that I see,
Poor fellow me.
Once I was gay,
Once I was gay,
Once I was gay,
Poor fellow me.
Then came the day,
I went away.
Now I am grey,
Poor fellow me.
Now I'm alone,
Now I'm alone,
Now I'm alone,
Poor fellow me.
Nothing I own,
Spirit has flown,
Poor fellow me.
So let me die,
Peaceful I lie,
Let my shade fly,
Poor fellow me.
Poor fellow me.

Bill Harney loved Ayers Rock. For many visitors he WAS the Rock—hard, weathered, rich with the wisdom of many years and much pain. Now he is gone. But the monolith remains, ageless and immutable.

People of the Centre

IN THE YARD of the Alice Springs railway station is a big stone, chained off, on which is a plaque inscribed: "This stone is mentioned in the legends of the Arunta tribe associated with the country around Alice Springs. It is Gnoilya (Wild Dog) Tmerga. This stone is associated with a great white dog man who came from Latrika away to the west and wanted to kill the dog men at Choritja (Stuart, or Alice Springs). When they saw him the local Gnoilya men sang out: 'Wunna meainda brinna numma—see, this is your camp. Sit down'.

"So he sat down quietly and remained there, the stone arising to mark the spot. If the stone is rubbed by the old men all the camp dogs begin to growl and grow fierce. The last man to rub it was one of the old Inkatas (headmen), who did so soon after the white men had come in order to try and make the dogs bite them . . ."

All the country around Alice Springs belonged to the Aranda (or as often spelled, Arunta), perhaps the greatest of the Aboriginal tribes, who once could muster a thousand warriors for some ceremonial corroborees. The Aranda still live around Alice and at Santa Teresa mission to the east and Hermannsburg to the west, as well as on nearby cattle stations. But their proud days are gone.

How long this great tribe and its neighbours—the Pitjantjaras, Loritjas, Pintubis, Wailbris and the rest—have lived in Central Australia, is a mystery. Some scientists say 50,000 years, some 100,000. All are agreed that it is a very long time. When the white man arrived he was greeted by the puny defiance of perhaps the most primitive people on earth. "We didn't conquer their land," a veteran pastoralist said. "We just moved in and took it."

LEFT: *Weapon in hand, this gnarled old warrior sits before a cleft which once sheltered his people.*

BELOW: *Aboriginal stockman helping to yard cattle near Alice Springs.*

The mica fields at Hartz Range, out from Alice, are idle now, but the local cattlemen can still hold a race meeting. And this old native makes the most of it by offering garnets for sale to visitors.

Brumbies at the Alice Springs annual rodeo give competitors as rough a ride as any they will have. Most local stockmen are skilful riders.

In their original state the Aborigines of the Centre built no houses, raised no crops. Their spears were little more than pointed sticks, but they had an extraordinary degree of skill in tracking and hunting prey. They wore nothing. Where they came from is a mystery, though most modern experts believe they originated somewhere in the islands north of Australia. Certainly they had been isolated from the mainstream of the human race for uncounted generations.

Yet the Aborigine had an extensive and elaborate social structure. Totemic rites linked him intimately with the secret world of myth and mystery. Only men could take part in the more important ceremonies and the oldest warriors were custodians of the tribe's secrets. Far from being unrestricted, life in all its aspects was disciplined by taboos, conventions and involved kinship rules. The strong and vigorous were bound to provide food for the old and feeble—except in time of famine when the aged and the very young were abandoned in the desert to die while the tribe moved on.

Within Aboriginal society death was the most significant event and relatives would mourn their loss with elaborate ritual. However, the people were neither gloomy nor oppressed with witchcraft. Singing and dancing were very much part of their lives. Around the fires at night men and women joined in "play" corroborees. Relations between the sexes were free before marriage and scarcely less so afterwards.

Life followed the pattern of the seasons. The women hunted lizards and foraged for yams and edible plants. The men speared wallabies on the plain, caught snakes beside the billabongs. They killed the wild turkey and ate its eggs and fought little wars with their neighbours. This stark but well-ordered round of existence came to an end with the arrival of the white men.

The vegetation of the country was marginal, with waterholes far apart and guarded jealously. As game declined in one area the people would move on to the next soak, maybe 150 kilometres away. During the drought years they suffered. Life was always hard, but with the influx of white settlers the traditional ways became impossible. Pastoralists took over the waterholes. Cattle poured in to the country, disturbing and driving away the natural game on which the tribes relied. Stock-killing was the inevitable response of the primitive

The field comes pounding round the bend in a cloud of dust at the Hartz Range races.

and faced with this the station owners, hard men trying to wrest a living from a hard land, reacted violently.

The people found themselves ordered away from their traditional waterholes and drought refuges at rifle point. Those who resisted were shot. Nomadic life was no longer practicable and the tribes began to break up. Some Aborigines settled around the stations, the men working as stockmen for their rations, the women as kitchen hands at the homesteads. Others drifted in to Alice Springs where they camped on the outskirts cadging food or bartering their wives for liquor.

A few fought back. In 1930 a white dingo trapper named Fred Brooks was murdered in his camp on Coniston station. Aborigines went on an orgy of cattle killing. When another white man—station owner William Morton—was clubbed nearly to death, Constable George Murray was sent to arrest the troublemakers.

He led what was in effect a punitive expedition. A judicial inquiry held later into what became known as "the Coniston massacre" revealed that thirty-one Aborigines were shot dead in two camps thirty miles apart.

Anmatjira tribesman George Jabaljari, who lives now at Mount Allen cattle station 270 kilometres west of Alice Springs, is one of the survivors. All his friends and relatives were killed in the massacre. George lived because as soon as he heard Brooks had been murdered and Morton attacked he realised there would be reprisals and decided to hunt well away from the main party. "They were bad times all right," he said recently. "All the tribes in this country were badly frightened."

It may have been the Coniston affair and others like it that sent a branch of the Pintubi tribe plodding westward to find a new home far from the influence of white men. Several hundred still live out there in the desert beyond Lake Mackay, wandering in clan groups, living mainly on lizards and rodents. Their waterholes often are soaks so poor it takes hours for a gallon of murky liquid to gather in the bottom. Sometimes they might go weeks without killing anything so big as a kangaroo. Only in the rare good seasons can they gather as a tribe for initiations and the great ceremonies which give meaning to their existence.

Bushmen have known for years of the Pintubis. Occasionally they called at Mount Doreen station

17

Limned against the sky like a sentinel from the vanished part of his people, an armed warrior watches from a vantage point in the MacDonnell Ranges.

A group of stockmen sit on their bedrolls at their camp on Two Wells station. They drink traditional billy tea and eat damper and a variety of foods which would have been unheard of in similar circumstances in pioneering days.

or at Balgo Hills mission over the West Australian border. But they did not achieve national prominence until the early 1950s when the late Bill Braitling, pioneer cattleman of Mount Doreen, told newsmen of the existence of the world's last Stone Age community.

Since then the Welfare Branch has made patrols into the Pintubi country, but the people show no sign of wanting to leave the desert. Everywhere else in the Centre the Aborigines are reaching out for canned foods, picture shows, houses . . . all the new goods and experiences the white men can give them. For some reason the Pintubis are different. They have neither accepted nor rejected civilisation. They have simply ignored it.

The pioneers cannot be judged by the standards of a softer generation. In most cases surrounded by an alien, often hostile people, far more numerous than themselves, they saw no alternative to the use of force. Indeed, many treated the Aborigines with great kindness, allowing them to kill a few bullocks each week for meat and issuing tea, flour and sugar in return for work around the station. Even the worst of the cattlemen were hard

rather than cruel. This was something the tribes could understand, for without toughness, physical and mental, no man could hope to survive in the desert.

During September 1905 F. R. George led a prospecting party to the Petermann Ranges. The sponsors, the Government of South Australia, ordered him to examine the area for minerals and then head north to Tanami, far out in the desert. With prospectors Hutton, Treloar, Fabian and Hall, camel driver Edginton and two natives, George pushed north-west from Oodnadatta. It was early summer, and apart from hidden soaks known only to the natives, the country was waterless.

Advancing slowly, taking specimens as they went, the prospectors moved toward the Petermanns. At first they managed to persuade wandering Aborigines to guide them to water. But after seeing the way George's camels fouled and damaged the little soaks, the tribes became hostile. On the night of December 6, painted warriors attacked the sleeping camp, spearing Hall in the eye and Fabian in the chest. George wrote in his journal: "Hall having the spear embedded in his

The Ross River school with its six students and one teacher.

the bush. He could read tracks like an aboriginal.

When Harold Bell Lasseter failed to return from the Petermann Ranges in 1931 after seeking his elusive "mountain of gold", it was Buck who went looking for him. He found Lasseter's body and buried it in the hills. For years Bob won rounds of drinks in Alice Springs by producing a set of teeth which he claimed were Lasseter's, and tossing them on to the bar counter at the Stuart Arms.

When on his station, "Doctor's Stones", out from Alice, he lived like a native in his mud house with fowls and goats wandering in and out. But his hospitality was enormous. Visitors were regaled with stories and mugs of rum. A few months before he died the old bushman said he "hoped none of the territory liars would stay away from his funeral". None did.

Not all of the early settlers were men. With them came some of the most remarkable women in the history of Australian pioneering. One was Mrs

Witchetty grubs are a delicacy among the Aborigines, who dig them from roots and fallen trees. Fat, white, juicy — the late bush raconteur Bill Harney compared the grubs with the large white snails and edible frogs of France. Obviously Bill has a disciple in this lad, whose eyes light up with eager anticipation of the treat.

head, we gave him first attention. He was in great agony and kept asking us to pull the spear out. Found it had sunk into the eye socket right below the barb. The attempt to cut the barb gave him so much pain that I had to release it by cutting the eyelid with a razor. Although in great agony, he bore it manfully."

Yet such was the toughness of these pioneers that within fifteen days both wounded men were fit to travel. Passing north of Mount Harris across the sandhills of Andoonderrina Well, George led his party to Haast Bluff and then toward Glen Helen where, after three months of suffering, they were greeted at the nearby cattle station with ample food and water. Most of the expedition stayed there to rest. But George, nearly blinded by an eye complaint, pushed on with Edginton and one native for Alice Springs, where he planned to catch the coach to Adelaide for medical treatment. They reached the Alice on March 31, 1906, but only a month later George died, his health broken by the desert trek.

One of the Centre's grand old bushmen and story-tellers was Bob Buck, who was well in his eighties when he died a few years ago. Friends said he was either born in the territory or chiselled straight from the MacDonnell Ranges. A large man with a round rubicund walrus-like face and massive moustache, Bob spent most of his life in

Character and strength are evident in the face of this desert tribesman.

Aboriginal stockmen of the Centre would rival Texans with their ten-gallon hats.

ABOVE: *An Aboriginal family on walkabout with their camels.*

LEFT: *No place in the outback is too small to hold a race meeting. And at Hartz Range the jockeys dress for the part.*

RIGHT: *The life of a desert prospector is hard . . . but Dan Sweeney could always raise a grin.*

Breaker teases the horse with a leafy bough while using his free hand to keep the rope taut.

Hayes, wife of the late cattle "king", Ted Hayes. She arrived in the territory with her parents the Doolans during 1905. They were a typical restless pioneering family of that era. Originally from Queensland, the Doolans followed Cooper's Creek down into South Australia via Maree. When the gold rush began to Arltunga they headed north again from Port Pirie and crossed the border into Central Australia, riding in a buggy which held all their possessions. One of their early camps was on Undoolya station, near Alice, where Mrs Hayes was to spend much of her later life.

When she first saw Alice Springs it was little more than a staging camp for the Afghan hawkers who used to stop there on their way up from South Australia with the camel trains. There were only five houses, yet the infant "town" boasted a brewery which helped to slake the thirst of miners on the Arltunga goldfields.

Mrs Hayes and her family drifted north to Newcastle Waters where her father worked for a time as a hawker. They bought a second buggy and she drove one of them, later riding along on horseback when the old buggy was sold. In 1910 she married a cattleman, Ted Hayes, and went to live at Undoolya. Over the years she watched Alice Springs grow from almost nothing into the thriving

town it is today, and became one of its most respected citizens.

The greatest hardship of the early settlers—men and women—was isolation. A broken leg, a cut turned septic, an attack of appendicitis—emergencies like these became matters of life and death when a journey of great distance on horseback lay between the patient and the nearest doctor. "What happened in those days when a man got sick?" an old pastoralist reminisced. "Why, he either got better, or he died. If he got better then he didn't need a doctor. If he died, well, the trip into town wouldn't have done him much good anyway."

One of the great social pioneers and the man who did much to end the handicap of distance was the late Rev. John Flynn—"Flynn of the Inland". He came to Central Australia in 1912 as a Presbyterian patrol padre with 650 square kilometres to cover on camel and horseback. So that women and children could have security in the outback, he founded his "Mantle of Safety" with an aerial medical service. This was made possible in the mid-1920s by Alfred Traeger, the Adelaide electrical engineer who developed the pedal wireless set. About ten years later Traeger invented the modern radio transceiver, now standard equip-

24

ment in every outback home, mission station and Government native settlement.

When John Flynn died aged seventy-one on May 5, 1951, seven of his Royal Flying Doctor Service bases had been established throughout the inland. Today the mercy flights reach the most remote parts of the territory, bringing swift medical attention to all who need it, regardless of race, wealth, or circumstances. This has been the greatest single factor in making normal home life possible on the stations.

As conditions improved for the settlers, so has the attitude to the Aborigines become far more tolerant. Missions, particularly the pioneer Lutheran station at Hermannsburg, helped to reverse the decline in population until now tribes are increasing rapidly. The Government provides health and education services and has an active policy of assimilation aimed at absorbing the Aborigines into the Australian community.

The main source of employment is still the cattle industry, and strict laws guarantee the coloured stockmen a wage and support for their families. Dressed in cowboy clothes and elastic-sided riding boots, they are a picturesque part of the Centre—

expert riders and horsebreakers, invaluable in a mustering camp. Few stations could get along without them.

Unhappily social acceptance moves more slowly. At the race meetings which are a characteristic event at even the smallest bush outposts, the Aborigine is prominent as spectator, and often as jockey. Yet he is seldom welcome in the bough shed where the pastoralists and their wives do their drinking. The barrier is even more apparent in Alice Springs, now a busy commercial and tourist centre with little time to spare for the coloured man. Nevertheless progress is being made. Some boys have received trade training as mechanics and carpenters, while girls have been trained as nurses and office workers. Youngsters of both sexes are going on to higher education.

While few share much social life with the whites, they do play football and basketball together, and friendships made on the sporting field often carry through into later life. Despite present difficulties the descendants of desert tribesmen have glimpsed a future of promise when they may hope to build a new way of life as friends and partners of the white men.

Stockmen and horses quench their thirst at a pool in the Trephina Gorge.

ABOVE: *The full beard and grave ridged eyebrows blend strangely with the white man's cast-off clothes.*

RIGHT: *The cool sparkling waters of Finke River as they pass through Ormiston Gorge.*

LEFT: *Aboriginal horseman . . . symbolic of the new life of his people.*

RIGHT: *Trees on the horizon appear to be swimming in water. This is the mirage, which more than once has lured men on to perish in the desert.*

The Aborigines of Central Australia are extraordinarily skilful trackers and hunters. Using their woomeras (throwing sticks) as aids they are able to hurl spears long distances very accurately.

The Best Dog in the World

"THE DINGO IS the best dog God ever put on earth. When they're tamed a child could pull 'em to pieces without danger. They're friendly, intelligent and faithful. But they have one fault. They're deadly killers . . . And so they have to go."

It was one-armed Peter Allen talking, the greatest dogger of them all. He and his sons Tom and Les are in the business of exterminating dingoes for the bounty. Yet though they have killed the beasts by the tens of thousands they love them too. The Allen's home ground is Central Australia, but occasionally they mosey over to Queensland or up to the Top End to give the locals some expert help.

Peter is an old man, gnarled and worn from his lifetime battle with the dingo. It was his father's trade before him and after service overseas in World War One Peter got down to it seriously. "I just sort of dropped on to the job," he said. "I wanted to master the dog and I couldn't stop until I did. As I tried to beat him, he'd beat me. I'd go on and on, experimenting all the time. But now I've got 'em absolutely whopped. If I set a trap for a dog now, I'll get him."

Peter, who has had a hook instead of a right arm ever since a horse "drug and tromped" him long ago, has been dogging for half a century. He has his own secret methods but also uses the steel-jawed government trap which is buried just under the surface on a dingo pad. Professionals in a dying trade, the Allens get caustic about some "amateurs" they have seen in action around the Alice. "They leave marks on the ground," Peter reckons. "Of course the dog knows something is wrong and walks around the trap. You can't underestimate him—he's cleverer than a lot of people."

The trap catches the dingo by the foot and many have chewed the limb off to get away. The number roaming the bush on three legs are proof of the animal's tenacity and courage. "The warrigal's got all the cunning in the world, particularly in sheep country where he is chased almost continually," Peter said. "The Queensland dog is particularly clever. Cross-breeding with other strains has made the dingo bigger, faster and more powerful. The bull terrier cross is the worst of all, because the bull terrier himself is a killer."

The Centre is one of Australia's worst areas for dingoes. They kill hundreds of lambs each year on the few sheep stations, and hunt in packs to cut calves out from the herd and pull them down. A bounty of two dollars for each tail brought in has attracted many men to trapping, though few keep at it for long. Pure-bred dingoes are rare and the regulations specify "wild dog". Inevitably some hard-up Centralians have been accused of scalping the camp mongrels.

The Centre has a strange and varied fauna . . . Frill-necked and mountain devil lizards, harmless miniatures of the mighty reptiles which walked the earth when Man, if he existed at all, was a monkey chattering in the trees . . . The great goanna, or perentie, growing up to seven feet long, which even civilised Aboriginals (and many whites) regard as a delicacy . . .

A saltwater crocodile basking in the shallows.

A family of wild geese. The gander mates for life, usually with two wives, and all three help with the chores of nest-building and rearing the brood.

This Northern frill-necked lizard is not nearly as ferocious as he looks.

The most numerous species in the Centre—indeed in all the territory—is the red kangaroo. In time of drought the hopping hordes come in from the desert, fouling waterholes and destroying valuable pasture. Most cattlemen shoot them on sight and there are fears that the kangaroo may one day become extinct unless strong measures are taken to protect him. The last long drought killed so many that it is now possible to travel a hundred miles or more through the Centre without seeing one.

The Red Heart has more than its share of introduced animals, some of them unmitigated nuisances. Camels, once the only means of transport in the desert, now run wild. Usually they stay far from the settled areas, ranging east through the Simpson Desert and down the Cooper, south to the salt lakes, and west to country where even today no white man has penetrated. Occasionally they wander into station lands, knocking down fences and upsetting cattle, and at such times they are slaughtered in ruthless camel hunts. But their favourite haunts are so remote and so inimical to other life that the "ships of the desert" seem likely to survive permanently as part of the inland scene.

So, despite all man can do to him, does the rabbit. The country around Alice Springs is mined and honeycombed with their burrows. The toll from myxomatosis was heavy, but a new disease-resistant strain has appeared and now rabbits are very much on the increase. In a land where pasture is so valuable they will soon be a menace again.

For some reason—either the climate or the long dry stretches—rabbits have never reached the Top End in any numbers, for which pastoralists in that part of the territory are everlastingly grateful. The Far North and the neighbouring Kimberley region do, however, have donkeys to contend with. Like the camels they are descendants of pack animals. Ousted by the petrol engine, the donkeys ran wild and bred in thousands. On some stations today they outnumber the cattle, competing with them for scarce feed and water.

On Victoria River Downs the problem is so serious that the management offers a fifty-cents bonus for every set of donkey ears brought in. Sometimes the payout for a year is more than $5,000. Along the Ord River shooters kill at least 12,000 annually, yet still the numbers increase.

The dingo is cunning, and a ruthless killer, well suited to his environment.

You see them everywhere; beside the road, among the scattered steers.

The Top End is the home of Australia's only real "big game". Along the coast from Kimberley to Queensland the saltwater crocodiles have thrived and multiplied since ancient times, growing fat on wildfowl, barramundi and an occasional careless native. Their age is a legend. In the hidden swamps of Arnhem Land are monsters which were old when the First Fleet landed in Sydney Cove. Sometimes they grow to an immense size. One shot near Borroloola years ago measured thirty-two feet from nose to tail, while specimens of seventeen feet and longer are not uncommon. All are brutal cowardly killers and man-eaters.

Early settlers killed crocs for fun but serious hide-hunting did not begin until the late 1940s. As the fashion trade clamoured for crocodile skins to make quality shoes, handbags, belts and wallets, the price soared beyond $2.50 an inch measured across the belly. The result was mass slaughter, and over the past two decades numbers have fallen sharply. Often the survivors were cunning veterans who were wise to men and guns and dived for the bottom the moment they saw a spotlight or heard the chug of a motor. Though shooting still goes on, nowadays it is no massacre but real hunting.

The largest wild animals in Australia are the buffaloes, descendants of work beasts imported from Asia for the British Army posts set up at Melville Island in 1824 and later at Raffles Bay

Donkeys were brought to the North as pack animals, years ago. Now their descendants run wild, fouling waterholes and disturbing cattle. Most stockmen shoot them on sight.

and Port Essington on Cobourg Peninsula, about 240 kilometres north-east of Darwin. The settlements failed and in 1849 the last of them, Port Essington, was abandoned, leaving the buffaloes to run wild. For more than thirty years they were undisturbed, the herds ever-increasing as they ranged south-west over the coastal savannah which is now their home. In those years they had no natural enemies, not even man, for until the arrival of European hunters the natives did not realise the beasts could be eaten.

Shooting began in the mid-1880s and during the next seventy years 500,000 of the heavy black hides were exported through Darwin. The first hunters worked on foot, stalking a herd until they were close enough to bring down one or two beasts from cover. As the other buffaloes fled the shooter would run after them, stopping at intervals to fire from the shoulder.

About the turn of the century men began hunting the buffalo on horseback, and over the years they developed a method that was cruel but efficient. The hunter, clutching the reins in one hand and a sawn-off rifle in the other, would spur alongside the pounding beast to fire at full gallop from a range of a few feet. He would aim for the spine, dropping the buffalo like a sack of potatoes.

These were dangerous moments when man and horse had to work as a team. The mount was trained to hold steady and then, at the sound of the shot, to swing clear of the falling body and gallop after a fresh victim. The process would be repeated until the plain was dotted with humps of quivering flesh.

The spine shot paralysed the beast, condemning it to hours of torture under a broiling sun before

Water buffaloes imported from Asia have multiplied to pest proportions in the northern regions. Their meat is now the basis of a large export business.

a bullet in the brain ended its suffering. While a hunter might knock over twenty buffaloes in a morning, the native skinners worked slowly, often lagging a day behind the shooter as they carefully removed the hides and took them back to camp to be salted and dried. Decomposition begins early in the tropics and the spine shot was adopted to put the beasts into agonising "cold storage" until their turn came under the knife.

The heyday of the industry was the early 1950s when for a time the price touched twenty cents a pound—about $14 for the hide of a mature bull. Some men cleared more than 10,000 dollars in a six-months season. The big money attracted a horde of newchum shooters whose inexpertly-cured hides gave the territory a bad reputation with the buyers in Singapore and London and in 1956 the market collapsed, suddenly and permanently.

A more serious threat to the buffaloes and other animals which wander among the quiet goose lagoons of the coastal savannah is the expansion of the pastoral industry. Fence-lines are encroaching and there is talk of shooting all the buffaloes to make way for cattle. Even the geese, which once filled the sky with their honking regiments at sunset, are dwindling as new roads open the plains

The Mountain Devil lizard of Central Australia avoids danger by changing colour to merge with his background. But who would want to eat him anyway?

to tourist hunters. The turkey or bustard, most succulent of wildfowl, is gone already from all but the most remote areas.

The hour is late but not too late for those in authority to declare the Alligator River country east of Darwin a national park, where beasts and birds may survive in their natural state. Such action must come soon if it is to save a living museum of Australian fauna from destruction.

Alice Springs now has annual camel races which attract large crowds. There are thousands of wild camels roaming the Centre.

Aerial view of the MacDonnell Ranges, looking like rows of trenches fashioned by some giant of the past.

West of The Alice

ALICE SPRINGS IS in the heart of the MacDonnell Ranges. Gnarled, twisted hills said to be one of the oldest geological formations on earth, they have been immortalised by the late Albert Namatjira and a thousand photographers and lesser water colourists. The main attractions which draw a multitude of tourists to the Centre each year lie west of Alice, where the Finke and other rivers have cut great chasms and gorges. Nowadays these streams flow only after rain and it is a rare year when the waters course through the entire length of the river bed to empty in Lake Eyre. Yet there is ample evidence that, long ago, permanent watercourses wound through a fertile land. Perhaps one day the desert may smile again through irrigation.

Heavitree Gap, Simpson's Gap and Standley Chasm are spectacular clefts in the ranges close to Alice. Farther out are Ellery, Serpentine, Ormiston and Glen Helen gorges; the "Painted Desert" and Mount Sonder; and south-west of Glen Helen Gosse's Bluff, a circle of ruined hills enclosing a crater where a meteor is said to have crashed to earth ages ago.

The area is a paradise for cameramen. Frequent limpid waterholes along the Finke and in Ormiston Gorge give off delightful reflections and shades of colour. The many residual formations include the "Vertical Rocks" and "Stonehenge" at Glen Helen and, toward Ormiston, the scalloped outline of Arunta Ridge. Mount Sonder, which the Aborigines call Urachipma, rises 1322 metres from the valley floor. It is the most distinctive of the central mountains and a favourite subject for artists.

In recent years a tourist lodge has been established at Glen Helen where the Finke passes

LEFT: *The "Dancing Girls", in the MacDonnell Ranges—rolling, undulating hills, churned into shape by some cataclysm of the past.*

BELOW: *The soft glow of sunrise on Mt. Sonder beyond the Finke River.*

Mount Sonder, and hills to the south.

Ormiston Gorge, with the humped shape of Mount Giles in the background.

through the main MacDonnell Range. Attractions close by include Window Rock and the strange vertical strata called the Organ Pipes. Serpentine Gorge to the east of Glen Helen has towering walls 60 metres high yet no more than 2.5 metres apart. Further down it opens up, with majestic colourful ramparts providing an entrance to the south.

Undoubtedly the greatest of all the gorges is Ormiston, 10 kilometres from Glen Helen Lodge. The spectacle is breathtaking, with cliffs rising many metres from the bed of Ormiston Creek, permanent water below, and above, the rock faces

Glen Helen tourist camp on the Finke River, with Mount Sonder in the background. Rain has given the Finke a rare flow of water.

changing from red to brown to purple as the day advances.

Tourism and cattle are the great standbys of Central Australia, but something more is needed if the area is ever to carry a large population. The mighty chasms of the MacDonnells long ago inspired the dream of building dams and irrigating the land for agriculture. Perhaps the most famous scheme was that of the late Dr J. J. C. Bradfield, a renowned construction engineer famed for his part in designing and supervising the building of the Sydney Harbor Bridge. He envisaged four great

irrigation schemes in Central Australia, combined with the harnessing of flood waters from coastal rivers to develop western Queensland.

In his paper, "Watering Inland Australia", Dr Bradfield wrote:

"Glen Helen Gorge, Simpson's Gap, the Finke River and the Valley of the Palms . . . would be suitable dam sites. Surveys and a comprehensive investigation are required to determine the best places, but the possibilities of a large irrigation system in the centre of Australia are apparent. The water may have to be conveyed from the reservoirs in pipes and concrete-lined channels to prevent it from seeping into the sand. The State of Bikaner, India, has run a concrete-lined canal into the Thar Desert, ninety miles long, and settled 200,000 people on a rainless area.

It would be possible to store in the many gorges the run-off from this area of 60,000 square miles between the MacDonnell and Musgrave Ranges, and impound enough water to irrigate at least 500 square miles of country in the heart of Australia with forty-eight inches of water annually. The water to be impounded for an irrigation area of 500 square miles would be 56,000 million cubic feet, which would represent a depth of seventy feet of water over an area of thirty square miles. There are gorges in the Musgrave and MacDonnell ranges where such dam sites exist and where a greater depth than seventy feet of water could be impounded, and others where water can be stored to a depth of 100 feet and over . . ."

The most recent water conservation scheme put

Gosse's Bluff, south-west of Glen Helen . . . a ring of eroded hills, showing clearly the crater where a meteor crashed to earth, eons ago.

forward for Central Australia is a weir across the Hugh River as it flows through the Waterhouse Range 72 kilometres by road south-west of Alice Springs. At its narrowest point the gap is only 137 metres wide from rock face to rock face at river level and its height would be over 60 metres.

The catchment area of the Hugh above the suggested weir site is more than 240 000 hectares, all located within rocky mountain ridges. With an annual run-off of 3.8 centimetres, which is a very conservative estimate, the dam intake would be around 123 000 megalitres. In this area the evaporation rate reaches 245 centimetres a year, so a storage 30.5 metres deep would last twelve years

if no rain fell—and the average annual rainfall of 22.8 centimetres is fairly reliable. Apart from the potential for agriculture, 1300 square kilometres of irrigated permanent pasture could add greatly to the Centre's stock-carrying capacity and safeguard and stabilise its productivity.

Dr Bradfield's original scheme was far-reaching. "We have rivers of sand 1600 kilometres long," he wrote. "These can be cleaned out and rehabilitated . . . Some inland streams subject to occasional heavy flooding could be dammed where there is a rocky bar, with earthen levees extending at an angle of forty-five degrees fanwise from the dam— each levee being, say, 225 kilometres long. Four

Pine Gap Space Station near Alice Springs looks like something out of science fiction.

A series of rock pools at the entrance of Ormiston Pound, looking towards Ormiston Gorge.

Ghost gums line a sandy stream bed at the entrance to Ormiston Gorge.

such schemes would provide a water surface of say, 52 000 square kilometres in so-called desert country when the floods came. The evaporation—245 centimetres—could cause a rainfall of 10 centimetres over 1 300 000 square kilometres of the dry inland. That rain, after refreshing the vegetation, would evaporate and fall again as rain . . ."

Dr Bradfield's ideas are controversial. Obviously large-scale water conservation would transform the Centre, but the huge expenditure involved must be considered on a national level and weighed against the needs and potential of other parts of the continent. However there is a pressing need for at least a small dam in the MacDonnells to contain the floodwaters of the Todd and Charles rivers which annually pour out through Heavitree Gap to dissipate in the desert. Otherwise the continued expansion of Alice Springs will soon become impossible.

Ormiston Gorge, north-east of Glen Helen tourist camp.

These tall palm trees are unique. Palm Valley is their sole refuge. They have probably adapted themselves to changing conditions over millions of years from life on the shores of an inland sea.
LEFT: *High sharp battlements known as the Organ Pipes are reflected in a waterhole on the Finke River.*

Boom Times in Alice

THE FACE OF Alice Springs has changed in recent years. The Pioneering Days with their tumbledown buildings, hitching posts and potholed streets have succumbed to the Twentieth Century. The very completeness of the transformation is staggering. Central Australia produces a big part of the territory's annual earnings of about $10,000,000 from cattle, but the pastoral industry, though still important to Alice, in no longer pre-eminent—transport and tourism play an increasing part.

Trucking firms tranship goods from the train at Alice Springs and run them 950 kilometres north to the railhead at Larrimah. As Darwin grows in size and importance, so the volume carried up the Stuart Highway increases year by year. By 1967 the traffic was worth $2,000,000 annually to the Centre. Now it would be much more. But while transport is a booming "growth" industry, by far the greatest influence on Alice Springs has been tourism.

Each year planes, trains, cars and buses pour into the town thousands of people—many times the normal population. The amount they spend must total millions of dollars, though estimates vary markedly. Tourism has provided a new and specialised market and a whole range of firms have opened up to cater for it. Modern arcades and shops reach a standard which would not disgrace the suburbs of Sydney or Melbourne. Restaurants feature continental cooking and goulash and wiener schnitzel are in the process of toppling the traditional "steak-and-eggs" from its pinnacle. Teenagers gather in espresso coffee bars. Everywhere the juke-boxes blare.

The changes must have puzzled Saidah Saidal who lived in the Old Timers' Home on the outskirts of town until his recent death. Saidah was the last of the Afghan hawkers who peddled their wares from station to station at the turn of the century. He came from Baluchistan on India's North-West frontier and was a boy of eighteen when he arrived in the Centre about 1896.

For thirty years he was a camel driver with the caravans which moved to and fro between the then railhead at Oodnadatta and the bush hamlet of Alice Springs. The camels carried huge pack-saddles filled with a bewildering variety of goods for the cattlemen and miners. When a gold rush began to Arltunga it was the "Ghans" who freighted in supplies. Even the crushing battery came by camel; it was dismantled at Oodnadatta, freighted north in small pieces and re-assembled on the site.

For years Saidah and his countrymen carried the materials to feed, clothe and even house settlers on the new frontier. Then the railway line struck north from Oodnadatta, roads cut through the

The work of well-known sculptor William Ricketts is a feature of Pitchi-Ritchi Estate, just outside Heavitree Gap at Alice Springs.

A colourful scene at the annual Henley-On-Todd Regatta held in the sandy bed of the Todd River.

The John Flynn Memorial Church at Alice Springs, a striking memorial to the founder of the Flying Doctor Service.

country, and soon camels were outdated. By the early 1930s their usefulness had passed, though their memory survives in "The Ghan", the modern train which now plies between Port Augusta and Alice Springs.

It was the only life Saidah knew, so he moved with his camels to South Australia, then took up work on the State borders, patrolling and patching the vermin fences. After years away he returned to Alice Springs and joined a tiny colony of his countrymen—all old—living among the half-castes at Heavitree Gap. Now he is a resident of the Old Timers' Home, established by the Australian Inland Mission as a refuge for homeless battlers who helped pioneer the territory.

Camels did a great job from the time they appeared in Australia about a century ago, until the motor vehicle took over. A pack team would cover 25 to 30 kilometres a day and a good riding beast might travel 160. Apart from the supply caravans they were widely used on stations, extending right over into the Kimberleys. The police took camels on their long desert patrols and only a few years ago they still had some on the strength.

A few kilometres out of Alice Springs is The

Bungalow, site of the original stone telegraph station built in 1871. The Post Office, barracks and block-houses are as solid today as they were ninety years ago and the area has been developed as a National Park and tourist attraction. Below the

Twin ghost gums on the route west of Alice Springs leading to Palm Valley, Glen Helen and Hermannsburg.

The Rock crouches like some prehistoric monster on the flat surface of the desert. Far away in the background are the Olgas, another phenomenon of the Centre.

Saidah Saidel, one of the last of the old Afghan camel drivers who once were a familiar sight in the outback.

The modern train which plies between Alice and Port Augusta is named "The Ghan", after those who went before.

Children at Bond Springs station talking to their teacher during a School of the Air lesson.

telegraph station is the Todd River with a deep, permanent pool in its bed—the original Alice Springs. Surveyor W. W. Mills discovered the place on March 11, 1871, during construction of the Overland Telegraph Line.

The present site of Alice Springs was surveyed in 1888 and the new town was named Stuart. Soon it had a race track, and a dance floor made of a piece of canvas forty feet by twenty, pegged taut and made slippery with boracic. When the Governor of South Australia, Sir Tom Bridges, came up with Sir Henry Barwell by horse and buggy for a visit, a reception was held in the gaol. The prisoners were taken out, the place was cleaned and decorated with greenery to hide the chains on the walls, and a big "Welcome" sign was raised over the cell doors.

On August 4, 1914, Mrs (later Dame) Ida Standley arrived to open the first school, teaching white children in the morning and half-castes in the afternoon. The railway reached Stuart in 1929 and not long afterward the town was re-named Alice Springs. The pastoral and mining industries flourished but the boom years really began with the war, when Alice was an important military base and the centre of civilian administration for the territory.

Servicemen spread word of the unique scenery and by 1950 the flow of visitors was under way. Bert Palmer, manager of the Central Australian

Tourist Bureau, says: "We get people out here from England who know only two Australian place-names. One is Sydney. The other is Alice Springs."

This is not really a cattle town any more. That Australian folk figure the drover who once enlivened the Alice with his fights and tall stories, has disappeared, replaced by giant motorised "road trains" which carry cattle to the railhead in a fraction of the time and without loss of condition. Aboriginal stockmen still cluster around the station outfitters and saddlery stores, but the bulk of the European shoppers head for the new arcades where Namatjira prints are offered side by side with native weapons (including boomerangs made in Switzerland) and other tourist curios.

Alice's 13,500 people live in a beautiful town of wide streets, leafy trees, colourful shrubs and gardens. Despite recurrent water shortages there is greenery everywhere. Several homes have their own swimming pools, fed by private bores. Houses, motels and hotels are ultra-modern. Togetherness is a way of life in Central Australia and nowhere is this more evident than in the Memorial Club. This unique institution with its lavish sporting and community facilities, dominates night life so completely that for many years the only social news carried in the local newspaper was an account of what happened at the club on Friday nights.

All this modernity has a vaguely unreal air. The annual flood of tourists has forced Alice, like the Mountain Devil lizard, to take on the protective colouring of a new environment. Beneath the veneer, however, traces of the old Alice linger. It is still, as it has always been, a home for "characters". Not least of these was Leo Corbet of Pitchi-Ritchi Estate just outside Heavitree Gap.

Leo was a man of choleric temper. Some years ago he was disturbed by the roar of heavy earth-moving equipment and looked from his front door to find government contractors quarrying busily into Heavitree Gap. Already a great scar was beginning to open up on one side of the natural rock gateway, which is among the most photographed tourist attractions in Alice Springs. Appalled by this desecration, Leo reacted typically. With the help of a legal friend he took out a miner's right and pegged the area as a gold-mining lease. Then he called on Police Inspector Bill

The view over Alice Springs from the north of the township looking towards Heavitree Gap.

During dry weather the Centre suffers from furious dust storms. Here an enormous brown cloud advances, enveloping the countryside.

ABOVE RIGHT: *The dust storm moves towards Alice Springs.*

LEFT: *A stockman admires one of the spectacular ghost gums in Trephina Gorge, out from the old Love's Creek homestead.*

RIGHT: *The driver of this Nissan Patrol Wagon pushes on through the blanket of dust, hoping to reach Alice while visibility lasts.*

RIGHT: *Simpson's Gap, a popular tourist attraction near Alice Springs.*

Alice Springs and Heavitree Gap, an opening in the MacDonnell Range to the south of the town.

Operators transmitting and receiving messages at the Flying Doctor service base at Alice Springs.

McKinnon and demanded the services of two constables to "eject all those people who are interfering with my mining lease". McKinnon was embarrassed but the law was clear. The quarrying ended and has never been resumed. Leo still held the mining lease and worked it the statutory one day a year, until he died in 1971.

The Corbet's home, "Pitchi-Ritchi", is set in spacious grounds. Originally built by the late C. H. Chapman who retired there after making a fortune from the Tanami goldfield, it is still as it was when Leo lived there, lived in and maintained by Mrs. Corbet.

It is a strange building with a sunroom and, surprisingly, a swimming pool poking out on top. The rooms inside, before Leo brightened the place with a few windows, originally had the appearance of subterranean passages. Chapman first built his house on a small scale then, when additions were needed, reacted like the miner he was, sinking a shaft here, making a drive there—all in solid concrete.

Leo Corbet, once a stock auctioneer in Victoria, came to the Centre in 1953 as driver-engineer for Dandenongs sculptor William Ricketts. "We were lucky nothing went wrong, because I'm hopeless mechanically," Leo said. "I wouldn't get a third engineer's ticket on a kerosene lamp." During this trip he fell in love with the Centre and lived the rest of his life there.

Ricketts, a nature lover who had been appalled at the desecration of the Dandenong Ranges outside Melbourne, made friends with the Arandas, Pitjantjaras and Loritjas. His work is difficult to judge, with human and animal figures intertwined. His own face, sharp-boned and a little over-civilised, appears often, and invariably his hands are reproduced as holders and creators of the strange scenes. His theme seems to be the oneness of Man with Nature and some of his heads of old tribesmen are magnificent. Aboriginal children peep out like hobgoblins in unexpected places. The several acres of grounds surrounding Corbet's Pitchi-Ritchi Estate feature an incomparable display of Ricketts' work, often set among fountains and flowers.

Pitchi-Ritchi is a bird sanctuary and hundreds

The Original Telegraph station at Bungalow, a few kilometres from Alice Springs. Built in 1871, it attracts visitors from all over the world. The old wagon (foreground) was used to haul supplies in the Centre nearly a century ago.

are present at all hours of the day including groups of the beautiful spinifex doves, so tame that visitors have to be careful not to tread on them. At the worst point of the drought a few years ago thousands of parrots and finches from the far outback descended on Pitchi-Ritchi. There was plenty of water but Leo had nothing to feed them on. At first a local baker allowed him to visit the bakery between seven and eight each morning to sweep up. He would collect half a bran bag full of crumbs and take it back to Pitchi-Ritchi. When this arrangement fell through he wrote to four southern newspapers appealing for bird seed. "I hoped some of the old ladies who keep canaries and lovebirds might oblige with a few packets," he said. Several days later a Trans-Australia Airlines van called at Pitchi-Ritchi. The driver told Leo: "There's a load of bird seed in the back and another two-and-a-half tons to come."

At the same time the phone was ringing. The Postmaster was on the other end of the line. Birdseed had been arriving by mail—bushels of it—coming in bags and packets. Many containers had broken and there was birdseed all over the Post Office. This had caused a plague of mice. The little creatures were burrowing everywhere among the letters and registered mail and the Postmaster was frantic.

Summoned to the scene, Leo shovelled a mixture of birdseed and mice into the back of a truck. It was about this time that someone christened him "the modern Saint Francis of Assissi". He thought it was "a wonderful compliment".

Alice has fine schools and sporting facilities. Its Youth Centres thrive, with hundreds of members. Traeger Park—named after the inventor of the pedal wireless—is by far the best sporting arena in the Northern Territory. The John Flynn Memorial

River gums at the entrance to Simpson's Gap, a few kilometres west of Alice Springs.

River red gums and red rocks in the entrance to Standley's Chasm.

The drover, a sunburned, wide-hatted folk hero, has almost disappeared from the Centre. In his place huge road trains rush cattle to the Alice Springs railhead quickly and without loss of condition.

Branding cattle at Tilmouth yards.

Church must be the most photographed in the Commonwealth.

Though not a large town, Alice has the "feel" of a city. It is the outlet for 200 000 square kilometres of pastoral country; the hub of Flynn of the Inland's "mantle of safety". It is the centre for the unique radio School of the Air, which helps bring education to children in remote areas. In Alice you feel you are in the middle of things, socially as well as geographically.

Such organisations as the Chamber of Commerce flourish. So do local festivals, including the Bangtail Muster (an annual pageant depicting the progress of Alice from pioneering days to the present) and Henley-on-Todd, an odd sort of regatta during which "boats" equipped with sails and wheels race down the dry bed of the river, powered by teams of sweating citizens.

All this is good for tourism—and good for the town too. Community life is healthy and future progress seems assured. There are fringe industries with profit potential: Vic and Sue de Fontenay run a date plantation; veteran Territorian Jack Swanson mines Australia's purest salt (97.9 per cent) from the bed of Lake Amadeus, a saltpan 130 kilometres long in sandhill country north of Ayers Rock; market gardeners in Alice itself grow

The grave of Rev. John Flynn — Flynn of the Inland — near Mount Gillen, a few miles from the Alice. His ashes are beneath an eight-ton boulder taken from the famous Devil's Marbles.

fruit and vegetables second to none when the water is available.

On the debit side, mining is in eclipse: Arltunga has long been a ghost town; Hartz Range mica is not worth working in the face of cheap imports from India. The cattle industry is always vulnerable to recurring droughts though now it is booming after successive years of good rain. The shortage of surface water inhibits any spectacular expansion of population and resources, the cattle numbers included.

The cream of the boom years may be over. Now the stage is set for steady, if unspectacular growth. But the Centre may have an ace up its sleeve. Out in the Simpson Desert Australian and American prospectors are searching. Already oil and gas has been found at the southern end of the Simpson, and some of the gas is being piped to Adelaide. Gas in large quantities has been found at Mereenue south-west of Alice Springs. However contracts written for its export to the U.S.A. are currently being blocked by the Government.

Massive sand dunes running parallel north and south to infinity in the Simpson Desert.

Resort with a Difference

A RESORT WITH A difference has grown up around the old Bloomfield homestead at Love's Creek, about 80 kilometres east of Alice Springs. This is pastoral country, taken up late last century, but the "working" headquarters of the station has been moved to Atnarpa. The original homestead, dating from 1896, is now the centre of a chalet which combines many of the features of a "dude ranch".

Love's Creek could be the forerunner of a new wave in Centralian tourism. The unique scenery of the Ross River region is still the main attraction but there must be many city people who would welcome—and pay good money for—the opportunity to ride a horse in open country, work cattle, and learn the techniques of the bushman—that remote figure who is still the basis of the Australian legend.

Visitors can travel through the surrounding country by coach or on horseback. Nearby features include the rock paintings and carving in N'Dhala Gorge and the Valley of the Eagles where great wedgetails soar overhead or rest on rock ledges. Further out is Trephina Gorge, every bit as spectacular as the better known chasms west of Alice.

Less than 30 kilometres from Love's Creeks is Arltunga, once the centre of a gold rush but now a ghost town, rich in memories but without one permanent resident. The country around is singularly dry and barren and the only stock it ever carried were a few goats which the miners kept for milk years ago. J. Byrnes founded the place when he discovered alluvial gold in the area during 1897. A mild rush began and Arltunga blossomed overnight. At one time several hundred diggers were working on the field. Lack of water, even from bores, hampered the operation. While a few men did well most found only thirst, sickness and death. The field survived fitfully until 1907 but production over the ten years was a mere 20 000 grams of gold, worth $55,000.

A visitor in 1942 found records of claims and crushing figures from the "MacDonnell Ranges Government Battery and Cyanide Works". These were still stacked neatly in the manager's safe as if the government, which evacuated its battery staff decades before, had hoped to return some day. In recent years souvenir hunters have stripped the place of everything moveable, leaving only the shells of buildings crumbling quietly in the fierce desert heat.

One of the real Alice Springs old-timers is Mrs L. Bloomfield, whose husband Lou took up Love's Creek station in 1910 and brought his bride there the following year. It was no paradise for tourists then. "After we were married we started for our home by buggy and horse from Oodnadatta, taking thirteen to fourteen days, camping out at night, cooking by campfire," she recalled. "Over the years we made the journey many times back and forth. We sometimes ran into heavy rain which caused the creeks to flood. Very often they were impassable and we would pull up and camp on high ground until the floods went down. On one occasion I was

Weathered blocks of red rock in the Valley of Eagles, named after the giant wedge-tail eagles found there.

Mount Undoolya when it is seen in the last rays of sunlight glows like an ingot of newly smelted metal.

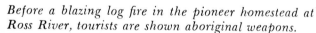

Before a blazing log fire in the pioneer homestead at Ross River, tourists are shown aboriginal weapons.

a month on the track with a young baby and another toddler.

"Our home was one stone room with a verandah closed in with slabs for bedroom and storeroom. The stones were dug out of hills, lime was burnt for mortar, and timber cut from along the creek. A hessian curtain attached to the door acted as a door screen, and cheese cloth was tacked over the windows, because there always seemed to be flies.

"Soon after we arrived my husband had to go away for a fortnight. I was alone in an unknown land with only a native girl, Ruby, to help me get used to the bush. I had no idea where my husband had gone. I would see a big dust cloud made by stock coming into water. I would shout: 'Here comes the Boss.' Each time, though the clouds appeared in every direction, my faithful lubra would reply: 'No, no, him come other way.'

"My home had no locks but I was never nervous. I liked the calls of the night birds but oh, the howl of the dingoes to me was blood-curdling. Water had to be pulled up from a well by buckets and windlass and carried to the house—quite a distance. We were fortunate in having a very strong native woman who looked after the cows and goats. She could carry three buckets of water, one on her head and one in each hand. Polly was a good old scout; she could drag a cow into the bail without any trouble if need be.

"Oodnadatta, our nearest railway, 650 kilometres away, meant also the nearest doctor or nurse. All our stores were brought by camels taking five to six weeks. It was a day of days when they came along. Not so exciting, though, when most of the lighting kerosene had leaked away and I had to go on with a slush lamp made of a tin three-parts filled with sand and topped up with fat. To brighten it up we poured in more fat.

"We broke in herd cows for milking, season permitting. No refrigeration of course, but a cool bush safe made from timber and bags, kept wet; and a water bag in a draughty place for drinking. The mail came every month—eight weeks before we had replies to our letters from Adelaide.

"When I was expecting a baby I had to go to Oodnadatta to the nearest doctor. After the baby grew stronger I would come home, camping out in all kinds of weather. Babies stood up to it all very well. They loved the motion of the buggy and horses jogging along. Callers were few—mostly prospectors or camel drivers. My nearest neighbour was a woman, 50 kilometres away. She, too, had

Thirsty stockmen quench their thirst with billy tea in the shade of river red gums in Trephina Gorge.

The beauty of the Centre after rain . . . Mass display of wildflowers at Palm Valley, with Sundial Rock looming in the background.

Many families live in startling isolation on stations in Central Australia. Todd River homestead is shown here.

children to care for and we seldom saw each other.

"Christmas was a big day for our native staff as Christmas puddings cooked in cloth, cakes, lollies, new dresses, shirts, trousers, bright handkerchiefs, tobacco and new pipes were prepared as a treat for all. The people would gradually make their way from walkabouts to come home for Christmas. If a native was sick we did what we could to help him but never got credit for curing him. It was always their own doctor who drew a bone from that particular spot. I never saw the wound, but have seen the bone of kangaroo or rabbit that did the damage.

"There is little now for us old-timers to do. Things have gone ahead. Time replaced the camels with motor transport and cars put the horse and buggy out of business. The railway came to the Centre and the first train caused great excitement. My family took an old native woman from the station in to Alice Springs to see it. By the time they arrived the train had returned to Oodnadatta. Later I asked what she thought of the train . . . 'I no been see him; only his tracks', was her answer.

"Oh well, time creeps on. My sight is getting dim. Things have gone on, leaving memories of the past, but it was all worth while."

The Loveliest Valley

PALM VALLEY, ABOUT 130 kilometres west of Alice Springs, is the loveliest valley in the Centre. Its beauty is of the inland, for there is no grass underfoot—only red sand. The rock pools are empty through much of the year, but for months after rain they are brimming with clear water. Isolated in the deep-walled gully are two varieties of palms.

The cycads, short-stemmed but long-leaved, grow among fallen rocks, on ledges, and in crevices in the cliffs where even a daring climber would hesitate to go. Cycads are found in other parts of the territory, notably at Standley Chasm, but their neighbours at Palm Valley, the *Livistona Mariae,* grow nowhere else.

The tallest of these graceful trees wave more than 30 metres above the ground and are estimated to be at least 5,000 years old. Even the "babies" only a metre in height may date back for centuries.

A million years ago, perhaps, *Livistonas* swayed by the shores of an inland sea. Now this oasis is the palm's solitary refuge.

A curious feature of the *Livistona* is a spiral curve in the trunk, often close to the top. Scattered among the palms are Ghost Gums, contrasting boldly with the deep brown of the cliffs. Ernest Giles discovered the valley in 1872 during his first expedition into the interior. He named it the Glen of Palms. But McDouall Stuart—first man to cross Australia from south to north, and a hero in the Centre to this day—may have passed that way a decade earlier, for he mentions in his diary entry for April 12, 1861: ". . . We are camped at a good spring where I have found a remarkable palm tree with light green fronds ten feet long, having small leaves a quarter of an inch apart growing from each side and coming to a sharp point. They

An Aboriginal woman and her children "fishing" for mussels with their feet in a billabong on the fringe of Arnhem Land.

Palm trees soar above the rocks in Palm Valley — an oasis of waterholes supporting heavy growth in an otherwise barren region.

spread out like the top of the grass-tree . . ." Another writer said of them: "The palms are as exclusive as princes, forming a close alliance amongst themselves and glorying in isolation."

Until the mid-1930s the valley was a regular camping ground for the Arandas, who wandered through this area. But with the advance of civilisation they abandoned the place and settled around Hermannsburg Mission a few kilometres to the north and at Alice Springs itself.

Palm Lodge, a tourist chalet, has been built facing into the group of rock formations known as the Ampitheatre. Features in this remarkable circle of stone have been named according to their shape: Battleship Rock, Cathedral Rock, Sundial Rock and Corroboree Rock. Once the Ampitheatre had great significance in Aranda legend and ceremonial.

Palm Valley was part of the vast territory of the Arandas before the white men came. Their first contacts with the settlers were violent and the tribe might have disappeared altogether but for the Lutheran pastors who established a mission at Hermannsburg, in the country of the western Arandas, just ninety years ago.

Sixteen missionaries with cattle, sheep and horses arrived in the area after a journey from South Australia which lasted more than a year. For three months they saw no natives but after a time the people appeared in small groups. Gradually the missionaries won their confidence. Apart from teaching the Gospel the pastors established a cattle industry and grew vegetables. Finally, with the aid of public donations in the south, they laid a pipeline bringing water to Hermannsburg from Kaporilja spring some kilometres away.

In 1877 when the missionaries arrived the western Arandas faced extinction. But selfless work backed up by health and education services gave the people confidence and reversed the decline in numbers until today they are increasing faster than any other tribe in the Centre.

In recent times the planned ordered advancement toward self-sufficiency and eventual social equality with the European has been disrupted by one man, Albert Namatjira. This painting genius of Central Australia, by attracting around him a group of followers and imitators, revolutionised the simple economy of the Arandas. His example showed them a way to make money quickly with (for many of them) a minimum of effort. The results were not always happy and drunkenness has become a serious problem at Hermannsburg.

Albert Namatjira was a remarkable man, not only for the quality of his art but because he was—and this is rare among his people—an innovator, a breaker of new ground. At a time when Aboriginal pride and dignity were at a low ebb he accepted the challenge of the white man and bested him in his own field of water-colour painting. He earned great sums of money and travelled far beyond his tribal lands. If in the process he destroyed himself, the tragedy was not Namatjira's alone, but one in which his people shared.

Albert was born in the bush near Hermannsburg about 1902. He revealed his artistry at an early age by making and decorating articles of mulga wood. To encourage him the mission supplied a poker-working machine and a platinum needle so he could outline the shapes of animals. Albert's work as an artist with timber was already well-known by the 1930s when water colourist Rex Battarbee visited the Centre.

When Namatjira saw Battarbee painting the harsh rock hills and desert scenery the Aranda knew so well, he was captivated. In 1936 the two men made a bargain. Albert would work as a camel boy for two months and guide the artist to likely spots. In return Battarbee would teach the Aranda how to paint. Thus began the career of one of the finest and most prolific water-colourists Australia —or the world—has known.

In twenty-two years of painting Namatjira produced 2,000 water colours—a tremendous output by any standards. Now that he is dead some have sold for thousands of dollars. Apart from his own work Albert has left a legacy of about twenty Aboriginal artists at Hermannsburg and in neighbouring areas. They include his five sons and a grand-daughter. In his lifetime Albert earned up to $8,000 a year, but under tribal law this was equally the property of a horde of shiftless relatives who battened on him wherever he went. He died penniless.

The tragedy of Namatjira is not the old simple story of exploitation of the black man by the white. As an artist his colour was an advantage—certainly as far as sales to tourists went. His dilemma was that of a man torn between two worlds but belonging to neither; attracted by birth and temperament to the tribe, but kept apart by his skill, training and economic success. Some say his disintegration as a personality began in 1954 when he was

The "Cathedral" rock formation — one of several in the amphitheatre of Palm Valley.

brought to Canberra for presentation to the Queen. This man of the desert, great artist but primitive human being, was feted in the south.

In the years that followed, Namatjira had great difficulty in controlling his income. The demands of his relatives increased, becoming a severe trial to his patience. Some of the tribal elders complained about this time that Albert was "getting proud", that success was turning his head. He made big money but seemed to be constantly in debt. The Aranda Arts Council, with Rex Battarbee as chairman, had been formed to help the Aboriginal painters market their work and budget their earnings. But it had no legislative power and at this stage was relatively helpless.

Namatjira began drinking heavily and formed a disreputable camp on Morris Soak a few kilometres

Many of the desert Aborigines are still nomadic. Those who have them use camels when they go on walkabout.

from Alice Springs. In 1958 rumours circulated that members of the tribe had pointed the bone at him because he had applied for, and been granted, citizenship rights.

During that year a drunken orgy at Morris Soak ended with the murder of a young Aboriginal woman. Soon afterward Namatjira, a citizen, was convicted of supplying liquor to a relative who was a ward of the Welfare Branch, legally barred from alcohol. The artist was sentenced to three months gaol but the authorities allowed him to serve the time on a native reserve and not in prison.

His cry as he left the court—"Why don't they kill us like dogs if they won't let us live as men?" —stirred sympathy everywhere. The Namatjira case was one of the main factors leading to the 1964 legislation which removed all restrictions, including those on liquor, from the lives of Aborigines in the Northern Territory.

Albert continued to paint at Haast Bluff and later at Hermannsburg, but disillusionment had set in. On August 8, 1959, he died in the Alice Springs Hospital. In mid-1961 Rex Battarbee launched a fund to erect a cairn at Hermannsburg in memory of Namatjira. Mr Paul Hasluck, at that time Minister for Territories, unveiled the memorial on July 22, 1962.

Namatjira painted the land he loved with a rich use of colour. Perhaps his greatest achievement was in breaking away from tribal traditionalism to attempt water-colour painting at all. The fact that almost invariably he confined himself to scenery and did not try figures, either human or animal, is a puzzling feature of his art. But as an innovator, the creator of a form new to his people, Namatjira's place is secure in any history of Aboriginal development in Central Australia.

He put aside completely the primitive art of his people. This, over most of the continent, had been concerned chiefly with the animals they ate, and with ritual and totemic symbols. Bark painting, which has been carried to a level of some sophistication along the territory's northern coast, was unknown in the Centre. Even rock painting appears in a modified form.

Cave paintings generally were done with charcoal, red ochre and ashes, mixed with animal fat. If a design had spiritual significance human blood also was used. The "brush" was a piece of soft

Benjamin Landara, one of the "Aranda school" of painters who grew up around Namatjira. They capture the bright, hard colours of their land with a force and clarity few white artists can equal.

wood or bark, frayed at the end. Sometimes the Aboriginal artist drew in outline, a quarter of an inch broad, filling the spaces with red and black lines.

In Central Australia, where the rock gives a very poor painting surface, the Aboriginal was forced to adapt what he had to his cultural needs. Instead of designs embodying animals and reptiles, the art of this area consisted mostly of concentric circles and parallel lines at various angles, although figures of men and animals do appear in the caves of Ayers Rock.

Namatjira was the first to break the traditional pattern. He learned to use the white man's water-colours—a difficult and alien medium—in two months. And he inspired other Arandas to emulate him, forming a unique school of artists who may develop in very different ways as the shadow of the master fades.

Writing in *The Month*, L. A. Bingham said: "Many critics of Namatjira and his fellow Aboriginal artists contend that they do not build on the culture of their own people, that their work remains an imitation of the West. It must be conceded, however, they they have infused into many of their paintings that which no white man could teach them—the deep aboriginal feeling for country and an innate sense of mysticism . . ."

73

74 *The weird shapes of the Olgas. These are the most obvious landmarks to be seen from Ayers Rock.*

Katajuta – 'Many Heads'

THE OLGAS, ABOUT 30 kilometres west of Ayers Rock, are a jumble of massive domed boulders, the largest of which, Mount Olga itself, dominates the skyline from every direction. The formation, known to the Aborigines as Katajuta or "many heads", covers an area 7.2 kilometres long and 4.8 kilometres across.

The first white man to see the Olgas was Ernest Giles on October 14, 1872, when he was exploring the George Gill Range to the north. He was unable to reach them because of the treacherous surface of Lake Amadeus, but in the following year he approached the strange formations from the south and rode right up to them.

He wrote: "The appearance of Mount Olga from this camp is truly wonderful. It displayed to our astonished eyes rounded minarets, giant cupolas and monstrous domes. There they have stood as huge memorials from the ancient times of earth, for ages, countless eons of ages since creation first had birth. Time, the old, the dim magician, has ineffectually laboured here. Though all the powers of oceans were at his command, Mount Olga remained as it was born."

Both Giles and Gosse estimated the central dome to be 450 metres high but more recent measurements by surveyors show the summit is 1069 metres above sea level and 600.5 metres above the surrounding plain—more than half as tall as again as Ayers Rock. The Olgas comprise twenty-eight separate domes. Some are isolated, others stand close to their neighbours, but almost all are separated by chasms extending to near ground level.

These clefts hold pools of good drinking water and because of this Katajuta has a wide variety of

TOP RIGHT: *Sunset . . . an outline in black against the orange glow.*
CENTRE: *Afternoon shadows gather around the Olgas.*
LOWER: *The pink glow of sunrise on the Olgas seen from Ayers Rock.*

plant and animal life. In old times the Aborigines would congregate here for their ceremonial corroborees. Now the tribes have given way to tourists who flock to the Olgas in thousands by bus and plane to wonder at the majestic spectacle and, frequently, to paint in oils and water-colours the stark patterns of the rocks. The great domes on the western face are about the same height and though they present a tougher climb than Ayers Rock many have been scaled.

The country around the Olgas and Ayers Rock is barren, but even harsher lands lie to the west among the Petermann Ranges—where Lasseter died. Most Australians have heard of Lasseter's Lost Reef, a legendary El Dorado somewhere in the Centralian desert which has held men's imagination for decades. The story first appeared in 1898 when the English magazine *Wide World* printed an erratic series of articles entitled "The Adventures of Louis de Rougemont of Bordeaux as told by himself". De Rougemont, exposed later

Some of the domes of the Mount Olga group rising at the end of the road from Ayers Rock.

as a liar and huckster, told of finding a "Mountain of Gold" in the Centre.

There matters rested until 1930, the onset of the great depression, when a former carpenter, Harold Bell Lasseter, aged thirty-seven, suddenly announced that he had discovered a "Mountain of Gold" while wandering in Central Australia years before. He persuaded some Sydney investors to equip an expedition and in July, 1930, headed west from Alice Springs to find his Lost Reef.

They travelled 560 kilometres to the West Australian border where Lasseter took two camels and went off by himself. No white man ever saw him alive again for he perished after his camels bolted in the Petermann Ranges. Bob Buck claimed to have found the body and buried it. A number of expeditions have since gone in search of "Lasseter's Lost Reef" but—if it ever existed—it is still out there in the desert, waiting for some adventurer to stumble on it and make his fortune.

Lasseter was not the only man to find tragedy instead of gold in the Centre. No-one ever mined successfully in the Petermanns, but an even grimmer prospect lay far to the north at Tanami, which is linked with Alice by a rough pad known as "Madman's Track". Allan A. Davidson discovered gold at Tanami in 1900 with a camel-equipped expedition founded by an English syndicate. The finding of two big rockholes nearby brought a rush of prospectors but the water was not permanent.

It was one of the world's loneliest fields, the nearest settlement then being Hall's Creek, 350 kilometres to the west. Water from the desert soaks was bitter and almost undrinkable. Many miners died of heat and exhaustion; others fell under the spears of the natives.

In April, 1910, a man named Pearce perished while trying to get from Tanami to Katherine. A month later heat and exhaustion killed J. Brannigan on the Tanami-Wave Hill track. Natives speared John Stewart while he was fossicking at Granite Hill, south-east of the original field. W. N. Frayne and Frederick Morris, both leaders of prospecting expeditions, died of thirst in the desert.

The Aborigines of the area were Pintubis, related to the nomads who still wander in the arid waste around Lake Mackay. Reprisals after the Stewart killing were so severe that ten years later

The smooth ramparts stand out like a monument raised by some vanished civilization.

the natives would run the moment they saw a white man; abandoning their fires, waterholes, sometimes even the young children.

But they could still be truculent on occasions. Noel Healy, who until recently ran a roadhouse at Dunmarra, was out in their country about 1927, cutting telegraph poles. Three loads had been gathered and there were two to go, and the natives were becoming very cheeky. In fact they had just kidnapped a black boy from the timber camp and killed him. One day at sundown about 500 came up, Wallamullas and Pintubis, and began hurling spears at Noel and his mate.

A few shots frightened them off but the whites left the area. "It was the only time natives ever put me off my camp," Healy said. He remembered the Pintubis as having blond hair—a feature noted by many anthropologists—grey-blue eyes and Hebrew noses, and he believed they were one of the lost tribes of Israel.

During 1909 there were sixty miners and 200 horses on the Tanami field which provided 28 300 grams of gold worth $8,000. The field was patchy but it kept up a varying output for many years. Only about fourteen prospectors were picking over the area, concentrated mainly at the Granites, south-east of Tanami, when C. H. Chapman began boring there for water in 1932. He struck ample supplies at 65 metres, thus ending the shortage which had held back development of the field. Gradually he acquired all the other leases, then installed a battery. No-one knows how much he made out of the Granites but it was a fortune, reputed to be in excess of $300,000. On one trip by car to Alice Springs he brought in $32,000 worth of gold packed in syrup tins. Chapman sold the Granites to a Melbourne company in 1952 and died at Alice Springs three years later.

One of the best-known prospectors in the territory, Jim Escreet, worked at Tanami for a while.

Ginda Ginda flowers growing near Mount Olga.

Legendary tales, most of them true, attach themselves to his name. For example, his method of driving off mosquitoes was to rub himself with a mixture of ant killer and dieldrin.

Better still was his way of beating ants which are the bane of most bush camps. As he described it, ants were no problem.

"What I do is bring some ants from one nest and put them on another, along with a bit of tucker. By and by they get to fighting. Well, I get a couple of day's peace during the battle, another couple while they're burying their dead and a couple more while they celebrate. After that I repeat the performance."

His long career was one of boom and bust. The best "boom" he had was when he and a partner made $50,000 out of Cox's Find near Laverton in West Australia. With two others, he sold the Granites goldfield for $10,000. Back about 1931 Jim was doing so well he decided to start an air mail run from Alice Springs to Birdum, the northern railhead. He and his partner ordered a plane from the south but the pilot crashed it twice on the way to Alice and once on landing. "We took a look at it and gave him what was left in lieu of wages," Escreet recalled. "You know, I never even got a ride in it."

Jim Escreet was born to a now dying profession. To be a prospector you must be a gambler,

South-west corner of Mount Olga. The regenerative power of rain is reflected here, with grass springing up around the skeletons of trees killed by long years of drought.

whereas today's emphasis is on security. You must be impervious to hardship and discomfort. Today's teenager reckons he is getting a bad deal if he cannot get Dad's car for the weekend, or if he has to work back for a few hours on a Friday night. So there won't be any more Jim Escreets.

His father was at the Hall's Creek gold rush in 1885 and at Coolgardie and Kalgoorlie seven years later. Jim prospected throughout Australia, New Guinea and the Dutch East Indies (now Indonesia). It was at Adelaide River south of Darwin that he was "rich for twelve hours". A geiger counter registered his claim as one of the richest uranium finds ever. But soon afterwards the instrument was found to be faulty and the ground worthless. He shrugged and went out to look for another strike.

Jim Escreet was as self-sufficient as any man ever was. He was well in his seventies when he was prospecting for tin with an Aboriginal couple. He was cooking, they were digging. After a couple of weeks the larder was dwindling and he told them they would have to cut out a "little bit sugar" and a "little bit tea". The old woman, Nelly, said: "Old man, why don't you go get that pension? Then we got plenty money."

"You know," said Jim, "I'd never even thought of it before." And that was how he finally came to apply for the old age pension. In the sixties he

Walpa Gorge divides two of the massive western domes of the Mount Olga group. Conglomerate boulders are strewn about the base.

was still active on the tin field at Mount Wells south of Darwin. He had a young partner to do the work and pulled his own weight by offering sage advice. When I last saw him he was planning to go south for the first time in years. For months he had been debating whether he should attend the Rugby League grand final in Sydney or the Melbourne Cup.

"You know," he said, savouring a pannikin of rum in his camp near the claim, "I think I might go to the two of them."

Australia's Grand Canyon

KING'S CANYON, A cleft in the George Gill Range 250 kilometres south-west of Alice, has only recently been opened to visitors. Its sheer walls of striking colour and immense size are comparable with America's Grand Canyon. At the head of the gorge is an oasis of deep rock pools supporting a lush display of cycads and undergrowth.

The track from Alice to King's Canyon covers a diversity of terrain, with more wild life than in others parts of the Centre. During 1872 Gosse, the explorer who discovered Ayers Rock, established a depot on King's Creek running through the gorge, which the Aborigines know as Watarka. Another who passed this way was Ali Blooch, a lean and cantankerous Afghan who came to Australia with camels for the Burke and Wills expedition and later was associated with the bush wanderer Duncan McIntyre.

McIntyre took part in the search for the explorer Ludwig Leichhardt who disappeared in 1848 while attempting to cross the continent from east to west, and in the Flinders River country far to the north he found trees marked "L" and horses. When he

lay dying in 1865 McIntyre asked Ali to go on and solve the mystery. The Afghan swore an oath and for more than twenty years he wandered North and Central Australia, often out bush for twelve months at a time. During the quest he trekked far to the south-west of Alice, and from his descriptions of the country it is certain he camped for a while in King's Canyon before pushing on into the desert.

During the 1880s when he had long been given up for dead, Ali Blooch rode his camels in to Powell Creek on the Overland Telegraph Line, claiming that while searching between there and Brunette Downs he had found a gidyea tree with Leichhardt's "L" mark. Nearby were four human skeletons, rusty buckles and other articles. Ali went on to Adelaide where he offered to guide a party to the scene but officials of the South Australian Government only laughed and the Afghan gave up his solitary quest in disgust.

Leichhardt's disappearance still is the great mystery of inland Australia. In April, 1848, he left Cogoon station west of the Darling Downs in

Heading into the Valley of the Winds at the Olgas.

The Olgas, a jumble of huge, domed boulders about twenty miles west of Ayers Rock. The tallest, Mount Olga itself, rises 545.63 metres from the surrounding plain.

Queensland, at the head of four other whites, two Aborigines, and a long column of horses, mules and camels. The country swallowed them up in its vastness and neither man nor beast was ever seen again.

The search went on for years; in a sense it continues today. Relics said to be of Leichhardt's party were found in the Gulf country, western New South Wales and Queensland, and in the Centre. Escaped convicts told of finding five skeletons and a number of carbines as far down the coast of Western Australia as Shark Bay. However the weight of evidence seems to indicate that the explorers perished somewhere in Central Australia.

John McDouall Stuart made several references in his journal to the possible presence of white men in the interior. In 1872, Sir Charles Todd, the Postmaster-General of South Australia who superintended construction of the Overland Telegraph Line, suggested that Leichhardt and his party may have perished east of Charlotte Waters, which is on the fringe of the Simpson Desert, just north of the border between South Australia and the Northern Territory. Natives had told pastoralists that a party of whites had been massacred in this region many years before. One account said they were attacked while bathing in a creek.

More conflicting evidence turned up in 1888 when the explorer David Lindsay discovered an "L" tree 100 kilometres north-east of Alice Springs. A year later W. G. Pledge found another "L" tree 320 kilometres further north. In 1896 the Hon David Carnegie reported finding among the Aborigines of Family Well, near the border of West and Central Australia, the lids of tin match-boxes, an iron tent-peg, a piece of a saddle-tree, a lump of glass, and tomahawks made of old iron, apparently part of a tyred dray wheel. He sent these articles to an expert, Mr J. Panton of Melbourne, who said they could have belonged to the Leichhardt party.

Expeditions "pinpointed" the death scene in areas as far apart as the Rawlinson Ranges in West

Mereenie drilling rig . . . The search for oil gives hope of new and exciting developments in Central Australia.

Looking from the head of King's Canyon, a mighty cleft in the George Gill's Range. The towering rock walls dwarf the trees below, which mark the course of King's Creek, known to the Aborigines as Watarka.

Australia and MacArthur River on the Gulf of Carpentaria. Drover Charles Harding found a plate inscribed "Ludwig Leichhardt 1848" attached to the charred butt of a rifle near Mount Inkerman, south-east of Sturt Creek and about 145 kilometres on the territory side of the West Australian border. A whole series of "wild white men" reported in various parts of the North were said to be either Leichhardt or his second-in-command Classen.

Whatever the truth, it seems unlikely to emerge now. More than 100 years have passed and Leichhardt's journal, whatever its hiding-place, would long since have crumbled. The pack animals are dust, together with their burdens; the iron is rusted away. Somewhere beneath the drifting surface of the inland, Leichhardt and his men rest quietly.

LEFT: *The head of King's Canyon.*

RIGHT: *Extreme pressure on the earth's surface produced this remarkably patterned anticline in the Krichauff Range.*

BELOW: *View toward the mouth of King's Canyon.*

Life in the Top End

To outsiders the Northern Territory can seem a strange place. Politically it is a colony, economically a parasite, racially a melting pot. The territory even has its own dialect: the inhabitants are not Australians but "Territorians". Maps may tell you the 1600 kilometre long black ribbon linking Darwin and Alice Springs is the Stuart Highway, but up here it is "The Track" or "The Bitumen".

Landmarks and townships along the way are referred to as "the 22-mile", "the 135-mile", and so on. Summer is "The Wet", winter "The Dry". Spring and autumn do not exist. Territorians don't take up farming, cattle raising, or croc shooting. They go out "on the rice", "on the cattle", "on the crocs". Alice Springs becomes "The Alice", Tennant Creek "The Tennant", Daly River "The Daly". The territory's northern half is the "Top End", the southern "The Centre".

The capital remains, of course, simply Darwin. Loved for its tolerance, its generosity, its free-and-easy camaraderie; condemned for its drunkenness, its inertia and its ugliness; there is no other place on earth quite like Darwin. This picture has been altered in recent years though, and some consider Darwin now to be an attractive modern city. The territory is a problem area. In its 1 300 000 square kilometres live barely 85,000 people, including 21,000 Aborigines, some thousands of half-castes, and big communities of Chinese, Malays and Filipinos.

Before the war the Northern Territory was a bawdy, swashbuckling receptacle for the nation's misfits—visionaries, adventurers of all kinds, men on the run; a refuge for maintenance-evading husbands. It was a place for people like Roger Jose, who went to remote Borroloola in the Gulf country fifty years ago to get away from civilisation.

LEFT: *Anthills grow up to fourteen feet high in the Top End of the Northern Territory.*

RIGHT: *The corner of Smith and Knuckey Streets in the heart of Darwin.*

He lived in an upturned tank with his lubra. (When his first wife died Roger, a practical man, married her sister.) He dosed himself with strychnine when he was ill, swigged rum, ate bandicoot, and lived out his philosophy: "Man's riches are the fewness of his wants."

Working out from Darwin were pearlers, sandalwood getters, trepangers, hide hunters. In the back country Wongo, Tuckiar and Nemarluk were planning and executing their ill-fated campaigns against the white men. The cattle industry was growing up. Out from Alice Springs men were pushing herds, founding new stations. Up around Victoria River Downs and back of Newcastle Waters, Mataranka and Katherine, mobs set out each year for the long, dusty haul into Queensland.

They were tough days. Former drover Matt Savage, when he was living in retirement at Alice Springs, recalled: "Up towards the Kimberleys a man with a reputation for being hard on blackfellows was paid a bonus. His job was to drive off the cattle spearers. Some used to shoot a few, but if you did, you didn't talk about it." Another veteran stockman, Nugget Raymond—last man alive who was at Katherine when Mrs Aeneas (*We of the Never-Never*) Gunn rode in more than half a century ago—remembers being surrounded in a hut, fighting off hordes of yelling natives, while spears rattled on the tin roof like hailstones.

Invariably the Aborigines were the losers. On the Daly River when Woolwongas murdered five prospectors the settlers turned on the nearest tribe, the Malak Malaks, and slaughtered most of their young men. George Conway, who once distinguished himself by riding his horse Commodore into the bar of the Mataranka Hotel, took part in a punitive expedition against Arnhem Land tribesmen during 1909.

He told the story: "There were two policemen, two other white men, thirteen natives and myself in the team. The others are all dead now. We were armed with rifles and revolvers and rode three hundred miles from the Roper across Arnhem Land to Caledon Bay and back. The blacks attacked us every night. We had to shoot hundreds of them. Some of their camps contained two or three thousand people. We didn't shoot for the love of it, but because we had to kill or be killed. There was a terrible row about it when the missionaries reported us. I was detained in Darwin for six weeks while a Commission of Inquiry was held, but it all blew over. Today there isn't a wild native left in Arnhem Land."

Even in town the guns kept banging away. It was notorious that no territory jury would convict anyone of anything. A man who shot a Chinese in a Darwin picture theatre was acquitted because, as the jury foreman put it, he had been aiming at someone else. Only a few years back when a man stood poised on top of a 100-feet-high water tower, drinkers at a nearby hotel laid bets on whether he would "chicken out". When he did jump wagers were totted up and money changed hands. Then everyone went calmly back to his beer.

The Stuart Highway, nearly 1600 kilometres of bitumen linking Alice with its administrative capital, Darwin.

The territory has changed since then. Darwin, Alice Springs and Katherine are bustling modern towns with most amenities. But the past has left its mark. To visitors the Territorian appears often as a ranting boozing tough guy, with a streak of the comedian thrown in. He is thirsty—drinking fifty-odd gallons of beer annually, more than twice the national average. Statistically, he is more likely than other Australians to kill someone, crash his car, go insane, get drunk, commit suicide, contract leprosy, write "rubber" cheques. On the credit side, he is generous. Appeals to charity up here invariably are over-subscribed. The Territorian is pugnacious but carries no grudges. He is tolerant on the subjects of religion and colour. He will suffer fools gladly. He is gregarious, amoral, no lover of authority.

These qualities, mostly born and nurtured in the bush, have rubbed off today even on the army of Public Service clerks who now are by far the biggest section of the work force. Behaviour which might get you certified down south passes unnoticed here. Cattleman Tex Mohr dances one-man corroborees and roars Aboriginal songs: "Ayayayayay . . . Ayay . . . WOooooOW!" One Darwin club has a member who eats raw eggs between beers. A well-known Centralian pastoralist was a prodigious trencherman who loved playing to the gallery in the dining room of the Hotel Alice Springs. Nicknamed "Alligator", he was reputed to have eaten an entire goat at one sitting. Nearly everyone has his act. A Darwin New Australian munches glass. An office worker eats paper. The result at times becomes a sort of Rabelaisian carnival to which tourists should—and in effect do —pay admission.

Even sport here is different from anywhere else in Australia. The territorian plays his football in The Wet, his cricket in The Dry. Because of sea wasps he swims only in winter and avoids the beaches from October to April. As in most of outback Australia, chronic lack of white women has given a male emphasis to social life. But more girls are coming north every year, attracted by high wages, a sense of adventure and the ease in getting husbands; and a healthier attitude is developing.

Marriage is frequent and early. The birthrate is zooming. Churches, sporting and other organisations work hard to keep young people happy and

The Devil's Marbles, formations of weathered granite boulders astride the Stuart Highway near Wauchope.

occupied and away from the bottle. Socially, the Territory year by year becomes less a rugged outpost and more a normal Australian community.

As the area grows "tamer" and amenities improve, more tourists are making the journey north from Alice to Darwin. The road they travel is the Stuart Highway, built during the war and maintained with loving care ever since; one of the finest driving surfaces in Australia. For the city-dweller the journey is one of surprise and fascination.

Roadhouses stand a few hours drive apart to refresh the traveller. About 16 kilometres north of Ti-Tree on the left-hand side of the highway is a cairn of rocks erected in 1960 and bearing a plaque inscribed: "John McDouall Stuart and William Kekwick ascended and named Mount Sturt on 23rd April, 1860." Later the name was changed to Central Mount Stuart to honour the Scottish-born explorer who left an indelible mark on this part of the continent.

Several kilometres back from the road, brooding on the skyline in that faint purple haze so typical of Central Australia, is the peak to which the plaque refers. Up there on the summit is the spot which Stuart and Kekwick calculated as the geographical centre of the continent more than 100 years ago.

Near Wauchope south of Tennant Creek are the Devil's Marbles, a relic of some prehistoric eruption, round boulders 12 metres through, hurled one on top of the other—many of them—in the middle of a desolate plain. Even a photo cannot describe the Devil's Marbles adequately. You have to see them.

Aboriginal corroboree dancers at Mandorah, across the bay from Darwin.

The Cutta Cutta caves have a range of remarkable formations for visitors to the cool limestone caverns near Katherine.

Tennant Creek, a third of the 1600 kilometres distance from Alice to Darwin, was once called "the ugliest town in the world". This is a libel, as anyone knows who has seen Camooweal or Marble Bar. But the Tennant isn't pretty. It's a mining town and looks it. The place got its start in 1926 when Aborigines picked up some gold-bearing rock in the area. The Depression started a "rush" and by 1935 several hundred miners were working on the field.

It was a rough town. Al McDonald, a veteran prospector, remembers a Canadian who had been shot in a street gun battle dying in his arms. The victim's last words were: "I should have got him, but the best man won." He was there too when Joe Kaminski and a partner named Bonney found the Peko, the great copper mine. They made $5,000 out of the first crushing and promptly sat down to celebrate. They began with a case of schnapps, drinking out of an empty tobacco tin, and they took only a week to go through the $5,000, with some of the wildest parties Tennant Creek has seen.

Most of the enormous wealth of gold the Ten-

nant has produced has found its way out along normal channels. But even in recent years there have been exceptions . . . like the two migrants who used the Government Battery at weekends to treat two tons of stolen ore, made a gold ingot weighing 2977 grams, divided it in two with an axe and vanished interstate.

Late in 1960 Commonwealth Police moved in after the Auditor-General, Mr Newman, told Federal Parliament that $36,000 worth of gold was missing from tailings on the Tennant field. The gold vanished from tailing dumps near the Government Battery. To extract the metal the thieves would have had to use a cyanide plant and the only one in the area belonged to the Government. If this was used—and it must have been—the theft was one of the most blatant in goldfields' history. The gold was never found, though one local came up with the inspired theory that "the wind must have blown it away".

The best-known resident of the town has been Jack Noble who found Noble's Nob, still one of Australia's greatest producing gold mines. He gave the bonanza away to a friend who was down on his luck. When he was over eighty he still did a bit of weekend fossicking, reckoning that there was more gold still underground than has ever been taken from it.

Elliott is the halfway mark between Alice and Darwin and here a number of stores, garages and a modern hotel-motel have been built. The success of the hotel-motel beside the track has meant the eclipse of the old Newcastle Waters Hotel, set quite a bit back from the road 24 kilometres further along. Newcastle Waters was steeped in violent legends. Stopping-off point for drovers from along the Murranji Track on the long haul through to Queensland, it saw some epic brawls. Now the hotel is closed, its licence transferred to Elliott.

On the road north to Katherine the hosteleries are many. Dunmarra has always been one of my favourite stopping places. Here, until its recent replacement with a modern garage-motel complex, Noel Healy and his wife built up their business in a garden setting. Healy is an engineer. Many years ago he started the first motor transport run in western Queensland and the territory and had "more fights than feeds" with resentful bullock drivers. He used his mechanical knowledge to build a refrigeration plant and claimed to sell "the coldest beer on the track".

Katherine, about 320 kilometres south of Darwin, draws its prosperity from the surrounding cattle stations, an abattoir, and more recently from tourism. About 30 kilometres from town is the Katherine Gorge where the river flows, clear and swift, between towering canyon walls. High up on the rocks are Aboriginal paintings in ochre. The fishing is excellent and despite the inroads of the hide hunters harmless freshwater crocodiles are still seen occasionally.

Until a few years ago the road to the gorge was a quagmire in the Wet and a dry bog of bulldust the rest of the time. Getting through was a job for four-wheel-drive vehicles only, and often took half a day. Now the road has been re-made, bringing the gorge within an easy half-hour's driving range of town.

Those who travel to Darwin over the Stuart Highway are seldom disappointed. Even today The Bitumen isn't to be taken all that lightly. No-one who has been stuck for hours with the sun temperature at 44 degrees will ever again fail to heed the veteran's advice always to take a few litres of water.

You have to watch out for cattle, kangaroos and wild donkeys all the way. North of Katherine you can add buffaloes and wild pigs to the list. A taxi driver at Pine Creek one night had to reverse at full speed for 400 metres when a buffalo charged his lights. The seriousness of these hazards is evidenced by the trail of wrecked cars (and empty bottles) which stretch in twin lines all the way from Alice Springs to Darwin.

But for all this, there are great compensations. Even mechanical trouble means nothing more than inconvenience, for no Territorian will see anyone stuck on the road without offering to help. The driving surface is good, stops for rest and refreshment frequent; beside which you find a mateship of the road which is like a breath of the old bush.

The Katherine River has cut a remarkably deep canyon for its passage. Fresh water crocodiles are quite numerous.

One of a series of rock drawings along the northern face of Katherine Gorge.

RIGHT: Boat parties below Jedda Rock in the Katherine Gorge. The rock is named after the Charles Chauvel movie, Jedda, which was filmed in the area.

BELOW: Darwin, seaport and capital of the Northern Territory, has grown into a well-planned modern city in the last decade.

Of course the territory is not only Darwin, Alice Springs, Tennant Creek, Katherine, and The Bitumen which binds them together. It is Sid Hawks' store, surrounded by empty bottles and prone stockmen on the morning of the Top Springs race meeting . . . It is the crack of a stockwhip along the Murranji, the droning corroboree song ("Poor feller me, poor feller me") and the clank of hobble chains as the native stockmen circle the cattle at night . . . The crack of a croc hunter's rifle along the South Alligator River . . . the line of spearmen heading out from Maningreda in Arnhem Land for a wallaby hunt . . . the honk of geese over abandoned paddy fields at Humpty Doo . . .

The Northern Territory is all these things and more. She is a hard, capricious mistress, but to those who love her well she is without peer.

Parrakeelya makes a splash of colour in the drab landscape. The thick, fleshy leaves hold enough moisture to keep cattle going through astonishingly long dry spells.

Gardens in the Desert

VEGETATION IN THE Northern Territory has a clear division between the "arid" flora of the Centre and the "wet" flora further north. As in the southern States, most trees on the plain are varieties of the acacia and eucalypt families. More than a hundred species of acacia grow in the territory, while the number of eucalypt types varies from about a dozen in the Centre to more than fifty in the North. Monarchs among the scrubbier inland trees are the stately ghost gums which stand like sentinels along the riverbanks.

Apart from the usual Australoid vegetation, one group of plants has links with the Indo-Malaya-China region. These include the banyan, with its mass of exposed roots, and the weirdly-shaped baobab, or bottle tree. Tamarinds and mangoes flourish along the northern coast and offshore islands while the mouths of rivers extend into vast mangrove swamps.

The territory plants as yet have little economic use. In the North some cypress pine, bloodwood and paperbark timbers are milled for local building, and around Alice Springs red gums have been cut for railway sleepers. The Top End Aborigines weave baskets and mats with fibres from the pandanus palm.

Above all else the territory is still cattle country and everywhere pastures are a major asset and topic of conversation. Strangely, much of the Far North, with its regular rainfall of around 150 centimetres a year, is poor grazing land. Annual downpours have leached most of the good from the soil and though the speargrass grows ten feet high during the Wet, it is rank and sour, with little nutriment for stock.

Extending right across the "middle" of the territory from Kimberley into Queensland is a belt of prime cattle country—open plain covered with Mitchell, Flinders, button grass and other pastures. Despite the distance from markets this is one of the finest pastoral areas in Australia.

With a railhead at Alice Springs the Centre has

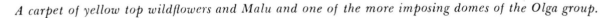

A carpet of yellow top wildflowers and Malu and one of the more imposing domes of the Olga group.

Arrangement of Northern Territory bush flowers.

no transport problems, but while the region has run up to 350,000 cattle, pastoralists fight an endless struggle against drought. Some areas have good water and pastures; in others the stock exist for long periods on saltbush, spinifex and mulga. The parrakeelia with its fleshy leaves can keep bullocks alive through many weeks without a drop of water, but their beef becomes very fat and greasy and often they tend to die from other causes than thirst.

The Centre in its more arid regions has all the appearances of a desert, yet given water it could be richly productive. After rain the bare earth beneath the mulga scrub becomes carpeted with Sturt's Desert Rose, wild orange, Pussy Tail, Poached Egg and White Paper Daisies . . . the white, gold, pink and purple of the transient wild-flowers. Sturt's Desert Pea spreads as a vine, covering the red clay with green then bursting into glorious crimson flowers; all within a few weeks.

Soon the earth is dry again, and only the withered stems and scattered papery blooms of these bright "everlastings" remain. But in the dust lie the hard seeds, which can survive drought and scorching heat and will again brighten the inland with colour.

ABOVE: *Wild orange* (Capparis Mitchellii).

RIGHT: Grevillea Juncifolea.

The Simpson Desert is a waste of dunes and bare red ground, yet even here grasses and a profusion of wildflowers appear after the rare rainstorms. E. A. Colson, who took advantage of a phenomenally good season in 1937 and became the first man to cross the desert eastward into Queensland, reported that the country looked like a garden, with water and pasture for his camels all the way. A few weeks after his passage the surface pools had dried and not a blade of grass was to be seen.

The soil of the Centre is rich. One of several men who have proved what can be grown around the Alice with irrigation is Mick Heenan, who has spent most of his life in the inland. He is that rare bird, a Centralian farmer. Using water from bores he became the Alice's first citrus orchardist, first poultry farmer and first commercial vegetable grower.

Parakeelya (Calandrina balonensis). *Cattle thrive on this small succulent because of its high moisture content.*

Sturt Peas, creeping across the ground as though weighed down by the lovely, drooping blooms.

The Sturt Desert Rose. This flower has been adopted as the floral emblem of the Northern Territory.

A clump of Poached Egg Daisies (Myriocephalus).

The opportunities for agriculture in the Centre are limited. Already the growing town of Alice Springs itself has placed severe strain on the underground water basins. But if ever the Bradfield scheme is put into effect so that wide areas can be irrigated from dams, the new farmers will owe much to pioneers like Mick Heenan.

Meanwhile the authorities could do worse than investigate the commercial possibilities of existing plants. One is the desert yam which grows in huge patches through the Centre. The tubers are thick and floury, tasting much like the domestic potato, and are a rich food source for the Aborigines. The plants die off during the long dry spells and come back in the same place after rain. The yam's keeping qualities are so good that an early settler once found a cave with hundreds of the tubers cached inside—the only known case where Aborigines have stored food for future use. Many bushmen prefer the desert yam to potatoes and more than one has suggested that the plants should be "farmed" and the tubers sold over the counter in Alice Springs.

Though good rains have fallen in the Centre during the past few seasons the area is still struggling to recover from what the territory's former Federal Member of Parliament, Jock Nelson, called "the worst drought in the time of the white man". From 1957 to 1962 no rain fell, and for the two years after that the storms were light and patchy, bringing on little re-growth. Between 1958 and mid-1962 the cattle population of the Centre fell from 353,174 to 176,617. The drop was not all due to deaths, though stock did perish in thousands. With road and rail transport readily available stations were able to move entire herds to agistment areas in South Australia. By late 1961 some properties were bare of cattle.

Despite widespread rains in the past two years re-stocking has gone slowly. The pleuro-prevention line running across the territory just above Tennant Creek prevents the Centre from getting its breeders out of the North, which otherwise would be the natural source. And they are just not available from South Australia in the numbers required.

The country will not recover completely for many years—if ever. Much of the mulga is dead

Rosy docks growing in the Flinders Ranges of South Australia.

Notoxglinon grows in rocky, dry situations and is common throughout the Northern Territory.

LEFT: *Pussy Tail* (Ptilotus Atriplicifolius).

and this is serious; when topfeed is gone bullocks can live for long periods on the foliage of the hardy desert trees, but mulga grows slowly. Even under the best of conditions the tree takes up to forty years to reach a size at which the trunk is seven inches thick. A veteran cattleman said: "The Centre needs a number of consecutive good years to regain its old vitality and I don't think its carrying capacity will ever be the same again."

Many blame the trouble, at least partly, on past over-stocking. During a run of good seasons extend-

ing over twenty years the cattle population built up to a peak of more than 353,000. Some pastoralists even indulged in the luxury of "picking markets"—holding back deliveries when prices were low and allowing herds to increase to dangerous levels.

There would be wide local support for a research programme to establish the effect and extent of wind erosion and sand encroachment and ways to arrest the process; whether and why there is a pattern of gradual drying-out of the Centre and how to prevent it; the extent and location of artesian basins and their rate of renewal; the ideal economic carrying capacity of marginal areas, and whether the weather pattern for inland Australia is changing.

Such a programme, undertaken over many years, would give a greater appreciation of the Centre's potential, and perhaps a warning that man should not attempt to wrest from the land more than Nature is prepared—and able— to give.

101

Opals, a Mixture of Light

OPALS ARE AMONG the loveliest of precious stones. Pliny the Elder once said of them: "In (opals) you shall see the living fire of the ruby, the glorious purple of the amethyst, the green seas of the emerald, all glittering together in an incredible mixture of light."

Alice Springs has had, for many years, fine collections of opals both for sale and display. Mrs Elsie Jenkins who ran the Ritz gallery in Alice Springs, had one of the finest collections in Australia— perhaps the world. Though her collection is no longer there, visitors can still find fine displays in the town.

In 1903 Charles Nettleton discovered the Lightning Ridge "knobbies"—ovate pieces of opal matrix embedded in jackets of soft white sandstone. The best of these stones, when cleaned, shaped and polished, reveal remarkable scintillating colours. Their fiery orange, red, blue and green lights are given a dramatic beauty by the dark hue of the base material from which they are refracted.

The miners at Lightning Ridge sent Mrs Jenkins and her husband, the late Mr Herb Jenkins— an early buyer of opals from the Lightning Ridge field—to England in 1925 with a collection of gems for the British Exhibition at Wembley.

Since then Mrs Jenkins helped make Alice Springs one of the opal centres of Australia; this being despite the fact that no-one has actually found a rich field in the district. Aborigines here and in other parts of the territory have brought in worthwhile stones and prospectors have found quantities of opalescent rock. Almost certainly a rich field exists somewhere and though no-one has found it yet, many men including amateur gem-hunters, are keeping up the search.

LEFT: *Repeating fold formations of the MacDonnell Range running to the west of Alice Springs.*

This cavern in Coober Pedy was carved out by miners in search of opals. Now it is a shop for selling opals.

LEFT: *The ant-like mounds of opal diggings at Coober Pedy.*

BELOW: *Working underground. The drill must be used carefully, otherwise a valuable stone could be chipped or broken.*

Many of the houses in Coober Pedy are underground ones. Cool in summer and warm in winter they are ideal for the climate.

Meanwhile opals continue to be found at the Lightning Ridge field in New South Wales and at various fields in northern South Australia. Coober Pedy and Andamooka are the two most important fields there.

Coober Pedy, on the lonely road linking Alice Springs with Port Augusta, is one of the world's strangest towns. The desert sun generates temperatures of 44 degrees and more and to escape the heat many of the inhabitants have gone underground. Homes and stores are found in caves tunnelled into the hills.

Yet they are well-appointed, for money is not scarce in Coober Pedy. The field has been worked for many years—old diggings stud the landscape like the craters of the moon. But there are still plenty of gems under the ground and rich strikes are made from time to time, often by newcomers.

Just what the opal search is all about is a story with an ancient beginning. Some 140 to 70 million years ago shells and bones were trapped within the desert igneous and sedimentary rocks of inland Australia.

Most of the original shell and bone was eventually dissolved leaving only hollow impressions. Occasionally at a later time, silica-bearing waters seeped into these gaps in the rock, hardening to form opal.

'Precious' opals display the valued points of colour flashing through the stone. It is the quality of the flash of colour which largely determines the value of the gemstone.

The opal was a very rare stone until the discoveries of large quantities in the isolated fields of Lightning Ridge, Coober Pedy, and the others.

What has been found nearer to Alice Springs is

Opals, cut and polished, are among the most beautiful of precious stones.

mica. A South Australian Government geologist, H. Y. L. Brown found mica in the Hartz Range 160 kilometres east-north-east of Alice in 1896. During the 1940s and 1950s the diggers numbered several hundred. Most were Italians and they took along their families, building huts of slab and galvanised iron. Then India flooded the market with cheap mica and the mines closed. Today it is a ghost town but the stations around still manage to hold a race meeting once a year and a few old prospectors still hope that "the mica will come back".